CROSSING RIVERS TAKING CITIES

Frank Damazio leads a large church that is impacting its community. An authentic man of God who lives what he preaches and writes from experience, he has successfully nurtured a prophetic spirit that is taking ground for Jesus through the supernatural power of the Holy Spirit. It is rare to see evangelism, pastoral care and intercession combined in grace to the measure that God has anointed Frank. This is a relevant message that touches deeply the heart of the Church.

MIKE BICKLE

MINISTRY DIRECTOR, FRIENDS OF THE BRIDEGROOM
SENIOR PASTOR, METRO CHRISTIAN FELLOWSHIP
OF KANSAS CITY
KANSAS CITY, MISSOURI

As Frank Damazio's father-in-law, I am pleased to recommend his latest book, *Crossing Rivers, Taking Cities*. The Church today is in a period of transition, and transitions can be fraught with dangers and problems as well as challenges and blessings. This book is about a man—Joshua—who made a successful transition for himself and his generation. He crossed the river and took cities for God. Frank provides plenty of spiritual lessons for today's Joshua generation of leaders to do the same.

KEVIN J. CONNER

WAVERLEY CHRISTIAN FELLOWSHIP
MELBOURNE, AUSTRALIA

I have long admired Pastor Frank Damazio's skill in extracting from Scripture revelatory insights that are utterly practical for those of us no longer satisfied with exotic theories. My admiration for his gift to take deep spiritual truths and apply them in his "workshop"—the local church—soars off the charts with his newest offering, *Crossing Rivers, Taking Cities*. I commend this to any pastor seriously considering the adventure of taking his city.

BISHOP JOSEPH L. GARLINGTON

SENIOR PASTOR, COVENANT CHURCH OF PITTSBURGH
PRESIDENT, RECONCILIATION!
AN INTERNATIONAL NETWORK OF CHURCHES AND MINISTRIES
PITTSBURGH, PENNSYLVANIA

Frank Damazio's *Crossing Rivers, Taking Cities* is a Holy Spirit-inspired blueprint for the Church at this hour. I urge you to take the plunge into God's river of revival through prayer and intercession as we seek to reclaim our cities.

JACK W. HAYFORD
SENIOR PASTOR, THE CHURCH ON THE WAY
VAN NUYS, CALIFORNIA

Frank Damazio's unwavering passion and vision to reach his city has always inspired me. The local church has a vital role to play in influencing its community and fulfilling the purposes of God. In this in-depth study of the Word of God, Frank has produced a book of significant substance that will ignite you to impact your city with the same zeal that characterized Joshua and Paul.

BRIAN HOUSTON
PRESIDENT, HILLSONGS AUSTRALIA
NATIONAL SUPERINTENDENT, ASSEMBLIES OF GOD IN AUSTRALIA
CASTLE HILL, AUSTRALIA

While many talk about revival, there are very few books that give you the how-to's. Frank Damazio has given us a rich treasure chest full of God's wisdom. If you are looking for a road map to revival, this book is for you.

CINDY JACOBS
COFOUNDER, GENERALS OF INTERCESSION
COLORADO SPRINGS, COLORADO

In *Crossing Rivers, Taking Cities*, Frank Damazio clearly articulates the Lord's heart to touch cities. He provides the leader, pastor and layperson alike with the goods to cross the river and impact their city for the Lord Jesus Christ.

MARK STRONG
PASTOR, LIFE CHANGE CHRISTIAN CENTER
PORTLAND, OREGON

If you're looking for fluffy, bedtime reading, don't get near *Crossing Rivers, Taking Cities*. Pastor Frank Damazio is one of the leaders of a new movement in the Church committed to radical intercession and aggressive outreach in these perilous times. You'll find his book a practical combat manual offering help to equip the individual believer and the local congregation to rise up, join the fray and conquer territory for the kingdom of God.

RON MEHL
PASTOR, BEAVERTON FOURSQUARE CHURCH
BEAVERTON, OREGON

Frank Damazio is among a small but growing group of clergymen who have come to understand that God has called them not only to a congregation, but also to a city. Although he uses the term "city taking," his book is really about community transformation. It is about replacing darkness with a full-bodied Kingdom atmosphere. Frank understands that for this to happen prayer must become preeminent over programs; pastors must become partners in a common vision rather than competitors for market share; and the heartbeat of the Church must be heard not only in sanctuaries but also in homes, schools and businesses.

GEORGE OTIS, JR.
FOUNDER AND PRESIDENT, THE SENTINEL GROUP
LYNNWOOD, WASHINGTON

Crossing Rivers, Taking Cities brings a much needed biblical perspective on impacting your city for Christ in today's post-Christian world. There is so much hype and foolishness in the name of revival that it has to grieve the heart of the Lord. Frank's words ring with a clarion intensity that desperately needs to be heard today.

TED ROBERTS
AUTHOR, *PURE DESIRE*
PASTOR, EAST HILL FOURSQUARE CHURCH
GRESHAM, OREGON

The only hope for America is the transforming power of the gospel of Jesus Christ. Frank Damazio believes that with all of his heart. Read this book and catch his vision for reaching your city for Christ!

LUIS PALAU

EVANGELIST, LUIS PALAU EVANGELISTIC ASSOCIATION
PORTLAND, OREGON

Frank Damazio uses the wisdom in the book of Joshua like a compass for spiritual success in taking whole cities for Christ. When you want to navigate a course for effective local evangelism, this is the book to read!

DUTCH SHEETS

AUTHOR, *INTERCESSORY PRAYER*
PASTOR, SPRINGS HARVEST FELLOWSHIP
COLORADO SPRINGS, COLORADO

"Has anybody seen my keys?" Frank Damazio has written a book that will help us find the missing keys that were misplaced during the Church's history—the same keys that were given to Peter and supposedly passed down through the ages. Only now are we rediscovering how by following the manifest presence of God we can cross mighty rivers on the shoulders of ministry. Thank you, Frank, for helping me find my keys!

TOMMY TENNEY

AUTHOR, *THE GOD CHASERS*
PINEVILLE, LOUISIANA

CROSSING RIVERS, TAKING CITIES

CROSSING
RIVERS
TAKING CITIES

Frank Damazio

LESSONS FROM JOSHUA ON REACHING
CITIES FOR CHRIST

Regal

A Division of Gospel Light
Ventura, California, U.S.A.

Published by Regal Books
A Division of Gospel Light
Ventura, California, U.S.A.
Printed in U.S.A.

All Scripture quotations are taken from the *New King James Version*. Copyright
© 1979, 1980, 1982 by Thomas Nelson, Inc. Publishers. Used by permission.
All rights reserved.

Cover Design by Kevin Keller
Interior Design by Rob Williams
Edited by Karen Kaufman

LIBRARY OF CONGRESS CATALOGING-IN-PUBLICATION DATA
Damazio, Frank.
    Crossing rivers, taking cities / Frank Damazio
        p.   cm.
    ISBN 0-8307-2392-7
    1. City churches.   2. Evangelistic work—Biblical teaching.
I. Title.
BV637.D35   1999   99-23086
269'.2—dc21   CIP

1 2 3 4 5 6 7 8 9 10 11 12 14 15 / 05 04 03 02   01 00 99

Rights for publishing this book in other languages are contracted by Gospel
Literature International (GLINT). GLINT also provides technical help for the
adaptation, translation and publishing of Bible study resources and books in
scores of languages worldwide. For further information, write to GLINT, P.O.
Box 4060, Ontario, CA 91761-1003, U.S.A. You may also send E-mail to
Glintint@aol.com, or visit their website at www.glint.org.

The City Bible Church Intercessors, 400 strong, who have persistently, faithfully and powerfully prayed for me personally, for my family, for our church and for our city. They have been my prayer shield, my prayer partners, my Aaron and Hur who have strengthened my hands during times of warfare. As we have focused on our city, we have encountered resistance, direct assaults, health problems and attacks upon key leaders. All of these attacks, however, have been courageously defeated by our prayer warriors who have stood in the gap, built up a hedge and, with bold tenacity, called on the name of the Lord, our Shield and Buckler and Mighty Man of War, who has taught us that the battle is the Lord's.

Our prayer pastors, Mark and Susan Jones, who like Charles Finney's prayer partner, Abel Clary, "Continued as long as I did and did not leave until I had left. He never appeared in public, but gave himself wholly to prayer."[1] Thank you, Mark and Susan, for your absolute dedication to prayer and to building a prayer army in our church.

Our prayer center lay pastors, Mike and Willa White, who model for the businessperson a pure-hearted focus on Christ, His Church, and His cause. You are both loyal friends and pillars in the life of City Bible Church. Thank you for your sacrifice.

Our young prayer intercessors, a new generation of young leaders— prayer warriors who, with heart, have caught the vision of revival and reaching cities. I especially want to honor Faith Prest, Lisa Elliot, Asim Trent, Rachelle Hjertstedt, Chelsea Smith, Kristen Riesterer, Steve Andes, Isaac Maddox and Peter DelVal, along with our generation ministries pastors, Doug and Donna Lasit. Thank you for your passion and vision for the future.

PASTOR FRANK DAMAZIO
FEBRUARY 1999

Note
1. John Maxwell, Partners in Prayer (Nashville: Thomas Nelson Publishers, 1996), p. 5.

TABLE OF
CONTENTS

Every authentic revival river has hidden within it stones to be carried out of that river. Revival stones are truths discovered and defined as we journey through revival rivers.

At Gilgal, we take off our shoes and allow our hearts to be circumcised. Our carnal strength must be cut away before we can supernaturally take Jericho.

Our cities are securely shut up because we have been fighting a high tech battle with a typewriter mentality! We need to upgrade our weapons of war and our strategies to use them.

Any city can be unlocked with the right keys and the right approach God's keys, however, are only given to the humble, the intercessors, the servant-driven churches.

The Church itself must be transformed before it can be a transformer. Dead, diseased, divided churches are impotent tools for transmitting Kingdom life to the city.

FOREWORD

Frank Damazio has given us a library of resource material in one book. A gifted Bible teacher and the pastor of one of America's great churches, Frank has gathered together a treasure trove of insights for today's spiritual leader. Drawing from revival streams worldwide and integrated with the great teaching themes of Scripture, this book is more than a good read; it is an extremely valuable reference for pastors and elders seeking to guide their congregations into the new century. Frank has outlined a comprehensive curriculum for tomorrow's leaders and gone a long way in covering the course. These pages contain an amazing density of content, lists of succinctly stated precepts that could be expanded into a lifetime of teaching by a pastor or Bible teacher looking for material.

This is a book about change—the change necessary to the American Church to survive and then thrive. Change is never easy, but it is always necessary. In Frank we have a proven leader, a modern Joshua who can show us the way. I appreciate the opportunity to learn from a pastor who serves his city, not just his congregation. Frank believes that transforming churches to reach cities is the foremost responsibility of spiritual leaders. He is an advocate for one of the most important shifts in thinking in the history of the Church.

Do you need hope and encouragement? This is a book for those of us who feel overwhelmed with the complexity of our times: leaders dealing with the moral confusion of our society, plus the many voices within the Church that compete for our attention. "The twenty-first century is here and it is ours," Frank boldly states, and he proceeds to lay out a balanced yet dynamic plan for congregational life based on years of experience, the best resources of the international Church and vast Bible knowledge.

As the pastor of a multigenerational, multiethnic church in a large American city, Frank has had to manage rapid change as the new generation enters into its inheritance in God. He has learned the things we need to know. When he looks at America, he sees a land filled with milk and honey but also occupied by a new breed of giants, a new kind of people, a new type of warfare and a new kind of church moving out into this new Canaan land. I believe that if we embrace the priorities so clearly stated in this book, we will inherit the revival and harvest that Jesus desires. For me, reading this book has been abundantly worthwhile.

John Dawson
Los Angeles

INTRODUCTION

I write this book as a pastor who is endeavoring to make a difference in my city. My journey has been marked by failures and successes, like most pastors in today's complex world. In this book you will not read the work of a creative author, but the toil of a pastor living out each page written. This is not a quick how-to manual on entering revival rivers and reaching your city for Christ. I'm not exactly sure how to live in the power of present revival or how exactly to reach a whole city or region for Christ. I am, however, sure of Christ's desire to move His Church into deeper waters and penetrate our cities with the gospel.

Therefore, this book is a window into our journey as a dedicated people who have embraced the ever-rising river of God to become students of crossing rivers for the sole purpose of reaching our cities. The biblical context for this book begins with Joshua as he models a successful ministry transition, passing the mantle from one generation (Moses) to the next (Joshua). From Joshua we move to the New Testament to examine city-reaching strategies, leaders and City Churches. I endeavor to weave together biblical thought with my church's personal journey.

At the end of each chapter, I have included a song written by our music ministry. These songs reflect our spiritual life and focus as a worshiping church. (If you desire further information about these songs, please contact City Bible Publishing, 9200 NE Fremont, Portland, Oregon 97220.)

Turbulent times, such as we live in, are opportunities for wise leaders to accomplish God's purposes. The crosscurrents within our culture that painfully resist everything Christ's Church is endeavoring to accomplish have given rise to many tensions. Tensions have also erupted because of traditional baggage that must be expelled lest we continue in a lesser state of spiritual fulfillment. Transitional times in church, culture and global economies call for leaders who cross rivers and reach cities.

I heard a young Generation Xer say something that caught my attention: "I have something to tell everybody. I've glimpsed the future and all I can say is, 'Go back!'"

Not me! Nope! Not now! We have come too far to go back. Besides, fear is no friend of mine or yours. We are people of faith and leaders who make transitions from one era to another. "After the death of Moses the servant of the Lord, it came to pass that the LORD spoke to Joshua the son of Nun, Moses' assistant, saying: 'Moses My servant is dead. Now therefore, arise, go over this Jordan, you and all this people, to the land which I am giving to them'" (Josh. 1:1,2).

As Joshua leaders, we are called to be vanguards, those who advance ahead into the future, forerunners, leaders who stand in the gap between two generations. In the Old Testament it was Joshua. In the New Testament it was John the Baptist. They emerged at the end of an era as it transitioned into a new time period. They were gap standers, forerunners, vanguards, those who held on to both the passing generation and the emerging generation. They were navigators into a new century. Today these are insightful pastor/leaders who see the emerging work of God and, with leadership skills, move people into the future.

City-reaching leaders know how to interpret the times, the spiritual climate, the prophetic signs and their own cultural contexts. However, it is not enough to simply know the signs of the times. City-reaching leadership must also know what to do about them.

Come, journey with me as we learn how to make ministry transitions, cross revival rivers and reach cities that are shut up to heaven tightly (see Josh. 6:1).

JOSHUA: THE BOOK
AND THE MAN

Ask of Me, and I will give You the nations for Your inheritance,
and the ends of the earth for Your possession.

PSALM 2:8

Joshua is a "link" book. It links the Pentateuch (the first 5 books of the Bible) with the next 12 historical books (Joshua to Esther) that cover Israel's history in Canaan. Within this history are the principles of divine teaching, nuggets of spiritual truth easily applied to a twenty-first-century setting. At a glance, the book of Joshua may be broken down into three sections:

Chapters 1–5   Entering the land of Canaan
Chapters 6–12   Overcoming the land of Canaan
Chapters 13–24   Occupying the land of Canaan

The first section will be our main point of interest, entering Canaan, the Promised Land, under the leadership of Joshua.

Joshua is a transitional book and the man Joshua is a transitional leader, moving from the Moses era into a new Joshua era, moving from the wilderness into the land of opportunity.

Reverend F. G. Marchant says,

> We may call the time during which Israel was ruled by Joshua and the succeeding judges the most secular period of sacred history. It is nonetheless important. The moral tone of the people who hear, and are called upon to practice what they hear, may be lower than it should be. The books giving the history of these people under Joshua and the various judges may be much taken up in recounting a history of failure and sin.[1]

This is a vivid description of the spiritual climate we too encounter and the challenge to become transitional leaders who move into the future.

"LINK" LEADERSHIP

The divine purpose of God was to successfully bring the children of Israel into their promised inheritance, the land of Canaan. The death of a great leader would not hinder their progress. God's plan is not dependent upon Moses or any other man. God has His leaders in training long before they are activated into the fullness of their calling. Joshua would be the Canaan leader as Moses was the wilderness leader. A new generation calls for new leadership, "link" leadership, those who have the ability to grasp the hands of the future generation without letting go of the previous generation. Joshua leadership moves the people of God successfully into the future without destroying the past.

In Christian hymnody and preaching, Canaan, the Promised

Land, has often symbolized heaven. This idea has biblical precedent in the fact that God's promise to "enter the land" was later interpreted as "entering the rest"—a rest from enemies and a full rest in the fulfillment of God's promises (see Num. 14:18-35; Ps. 95:11; Heb. 3:11; 4:3). In this book, Canaan is symbolically prophetic for those who are moving into the final great harvest of souls that is promised as we enter into our inheritance:

- Canaan represents a future unknown by the people of God (see Exod. 3:8; Deut. 33:28).
- Canaan represents a new leadership style and strategy to be progressively unfolded (see Deut. 6:10,11; Lev. 26:6).
- Canaan represents a new revelation of God's ways, presence, power and promises (see Deut. 11:10-12).
- Canaan represents a new level of strategic spiritual warfare (see Deut. 7:1-6; Eph. 6:10-17).
- Canaan represents a new strategy for God to reveal Himself to all nations (see Josh. 4:24).
- Canaan represents a revival harvest context with the crossing of the Jordan River (see Josh. 3:7-11).
- Canaan represents a model for city reaching that may be applied in principle to the Church of the twenty-first century (see Josh. 6:1-17).

"Moses My servant is dead" (Josh. 1:2). A closing of an era. An opening of a new time span with specific purposes of God. A new era, a new culture, a new vision, a new leadership style. Joshua would be the "link" leader, a transitional leader for the new future. Moses is dead. The old systems, the past methods, the way we did it before is passing. Like it or not, there is no turning back, no returning to the wilderness, no returning to Moses. He is dead. Pack up, move on. Leave what you must.

Take what you are allowed, but move on. Understand it. Embrace it. The Moses era has passed away with its systems, mind-sets and programs.

We must refuse to embalm the Moses system or seek to relive the past. The Moses system speaks of past methods, strategies, applications of truth and principles. We will never abandon eternal truths God has given for every generation to apply. It is the *application* that changes. Moses' Tabernacle was great for the wilderness, but in Paul's day, the New Covenant ushered in a new spiritual structure, the Church that Jesus is building.

Joshua leaders must be emptied of a Moses

mind-set. Just as Moses could not cross over

the Jordan, some ideas, philosophies and

strategies need to stay on this side of Jordan.

As Joshua leaders we must move from assistants to initiators and implementers. Joshua served as an assistant to Moses in an old system, with the ideas that were a part of that system. In the new system, Joshua sustained the truths of the old system, the Tabernacle of Moses, without building the future around that system. Joshua leaders must be emptied of a Moses mind-set in order to move into a new future with a new mind-set. Moses' mind-set was great for leaving Egypt and for the journey through the wilderness, but something had to change to go into Canaan. Joshua had to move from a "tabernacle" strategy to a "city-taking" strategy. Joshua leaders who maintain a Moses mind-set spiritually stagnate. Just as Moses could not pass over Jordan, some ideas, philosophies and strategies need to stay on this side of Jordan.

As we move into our Canaan, we need transitional leaders who will embrace whatever godly changes are needed to inherit the future. Change is never easy, but always necessary. With knowledge doubling every year, the only constant is change. The question is not, Will change occur? but, When and how will change occur? Global changes have forever altered the ministry of the Church. World events such as the end of communism in Russia, the disintegration of the Eastern Block and other socioeconomic and political trends demand our attention. The Church in America must face these realities and embrace them if we are to enter into the twenty-first century, a new millennium, with spiritual momentum, vision and purpose. We must make all necessary transitions.

Fighting New Giants for Fresh Milk and Honey

The land is filled with milk and honey. It is also occupied with a new breed of "giants" (Num. 13:33)—a new kind of people, a new type of warfare, and only a new kind of Church will affect this new Canaan land. George Barna delivers a wake-up slap for all leaders and churches as he makes the following observation with hard-hitting words of reality:

> Let's cut to the chase. After nearly two decades of studying Christian churches in America, I am convinced that the typical church as we know it today has a rapidly expiring shelf life. Our cultural norms, our personal expectations

and the condition of the Christian community at large have produced a dizzying array of challenges to churches. Across the nation, ministries of all sizes and shapes have responded with a frenzy of religious activity, producing more programs, buildings, events and resources than would have been imaginable at the turn of the century. Yet as we prepare to enter into a new century of ministry, we must address one inescapable conclusion. Despite the activity and chutzpah emanating from thousands of congregations, the Church in America is losing influence and adherents faster than any other major institution in the nation. Unless a radical solution for the revival of the Christian Church in the United States is adopted and implemented soon, the spiritual hunger of Americans will either go unmet or be satisfied by other faith groups.[2]

GOD COMMISSIONS HIS LEADERSHIP TRANSITIONS

Joshua 1:1 reads, "After the death of Moses the servant of the LORD, it came to pass that the LORD spoke to Joshua the son of Nun, Moses' assistant, saying...." Joshua was first Moses' assistant before he could become Israel's leader. All Joshua leaders must go through the school of leadership preparation if they are to be successful as transitional leaders. Joshua's success was based upon his extensive training under Moses. Past counsel with Moses had made him familiar with God's way and will. Past victories had given him confidence in his calling and faith in the supernatural. Past communication from God had pointed to his leadership and confirmed his destiny. Joshua was well prepared for the words to finally be uttered in his ears, "Arise, go over this Jordan" (Josh. 1:2).

We often do not discern success when it comes. We at times

do not fully understand our own journey timetables. When does preparation end and leadership in its maturity begin? Joshua must have felt insecure and inferior in his having to stand in Moses' place. He must have been incredibly emotional with a lot of second-guessing and doubting. *Can I do this? Is there anyone else ready who may be better equipped than I?* Here was a former slave replacing the great, educated Moses who was learned in all the wisdom of the Egyptians, who spoke face-to-face with God.

Perhaps you are like Joshua, a slave equipped to lead. Go on, for you may succeed when better men fail. But when success comes, don't forget the labor of your predecessors. As a transitional leader, you are harvesting where others have sowed: "Who then is Paul, and who is Apollos, but ministers through whom you believed, as the Lord gave to each one? I planted, Apollos watered, but God gave the increase. So then neither he who plants is anything, nor he who waters, but God who gives the increase" (1 Cor. 3:5-7). The tilling and sowing and weeding had been arduously completed by Moses.

GOD CHOOSES UNIQUE MEN FOR UNIQUE MOMENTS

Joshua was chosen for the task at hand. It was a unique moment for Israel: A long 40-year wait was finally ending as the Israelites were about to cross over. Joshua was prepared to be a crossing-over leader. God chose a leader according to the work to be accomplished.

To eject the Canaanites, a soldier was needed. For the Pentecostal sermon, impetuous Peter was chosen. For the great mission in Asia Minor and Southern Europe, ardent Paul. For the testimony on the plain of Dura, the three inflexible Hebrews. For the winning of favor from Artaxerxes, the devout yet courtly Nehemiah. The man and the emergency must correspond. Omnipotence never chooses to waste itself on human awkwardness. God cements things that fit.[3]

Joshua's resumé provides his unique fit for Israel's cross-over moment and gives us a preview of God's preparation process for the purpose Joshua was to fulfill:

- Joshua the warrior (Exod. 17:9-11).
- Joshua the servant (Exod. 24:13; 33:11).
- Joshua the faithful coworker (Exod. 32:17).
- Joshua the lover of God's house and God's presence (Exod. 33:11).
- Joshua a man of changed character (Num. 13:16).
- Joshua rejected by his brethren (Num. 14:6-12).
- Joshua received impartation through laying on of hands (Deut. 34:9; Num. 27:18).
- Joshua set before the priesthood (Num. 27:19).
- Joshua set before the congregation (Num. 27:19).
- Joshua receiving a commission (Num. 27:19).
- Joshua shouldering responsibility gradually (Num. 27:20).
- Joshua learning how to obtain guidance (Num. 27:21).
- Joshua the first to obey the command of God (Num. 27:15-23).
- Joshua an example to the congregation (Num. 32:12).
- Joshua consulting with the elders (Josh. 23:2).
- Joshua causing others to possess their inheritance (Deut. 1:38; Josh. 21:43-45).
- Joshua receiving encouragement from Moses (Deut. 3:21,22).

- Joshua receiving progressive revelation of his ministry (Exod. 17:14; Num. 27:17; Josh. 1:1-9).
- Joshua filled with the spirit of wisdom (Deut. 34:9).

Whom the Lord calls, He also qualifies. When He entrusts men with authority, He procures them respect. When He sends them into conflict, He secures their victory. When He gives them victory, He intends them to take possession. Now is the time for all Joshua leaders to take possession of the future. The twenty-first century is here, and it is ours. You may feel overwhelmed with the complexity of our day: the moral confusion, the values vacuum, and the demands on your ministry or leadership position. That is precisely why we as future leaders must take possession of and personally apply the promises given to Joshua.

As you read through the following promises, allow them to become rooted in your heart. Then get ready to uproot your doubts and launch out into your crossing.

- The Lord desires to speak to you personally and directly today, now (Josh. 1:1).
- The time is now to arise and go over your Jordan to seize the future (Josh. 1:2).
- The land is for the taking. Just walk. God will do the rest (Josh. 1:3).
- The boundary lines for your ministry have been set by God, not man (Josh. 1:4).
- The resistance will fade as you stand in your rightful place (Josh. 1:5).
- The attitude of faith and courage will be necessary to take the future (Josh. 1:6).
- The Word of God will be your compass in every decision and every conflict (Josh. 1:7).

- The blessing of success and fruitfulness will be yours as you obey the Word (Josh. 1:8).
- The ever-abiding presence of God will destroy fear and discouragement (Josh. 1:9).

All of My Breath
By Donna Lasit

Lord, I want to know you
More than ever before;
And, Lord, I have a thirst
That only can be filled by your presence, Lord.
All of my breath is yours
And all of my flesh,
I surrender.
Let everything within me
Please you, O Lord.
And all of my heart is yours
And all of my mind
Can see that everything within me
Longs to be filled by You.[4]

PERSONAL APPLICATION

1. To take possession of the new, we are often asked to let go of the former. Are your leadership strategies effective or merely familiar? What are some of the methods and mind-sets you struggle to leave on this side of the Jordan?
2. Take a moment to consider the ways God has prepared you for your next step of faith in leadership. Who has planted and watered and weeded so that you might

harvest? Do you have an attitude of gratitude?

3. All your experiences, including your delays and your disappointments, have been part of God's preparation for your leadership role. What "giant" lies do you need to overthrow in order to step into your authority and fulfill your destiny?

Notes

1. F. G. Marchant, *The Preacher's Complete Homiletic Commentary, Volume 5* (Grand Rapids: Baker Book House, 1996), p. 2.
2. George Barna, *The Second Coming of the Church* (Ventura, CA: Regal Books, 1998), p. 1.
3. Marchant, *The Preacher's Complete Homiletic Commentary*, p. 5.
4. Donna Lasit, "All of My Breath," City Bible Music, 1997. Used with permission.

CHAPTER 2

CROSSING
THE RIVERS OF GOD

Then Joshua rose early in the morning; and they set out from Acacia Grove and came to the Jordan, he and all the children of Israel, and lodged there before they crossed over.

JOSHUA 3:1

The Joshua leader is brought to the edge of Jordan, a river of destiny for the people of God. The crossing will draw a line in their history—a new day will dawn, a new purpose will unfold. The crossing of rivers and the taking of Canaan has always been the call for the people of God. Israel's Canaan had walled cities, numerous gods, temples and cultic practices. All were to be rooted out.

We also stand on the edge of a river ready to cross over into our Canaan—into a future with walled cities, pagan religions and immoral cultic worship of human-made gods. Our Canaan is actually very similar to Joshua's Canaan, a land with many gods.

Too Many Gods, Not One Lord

Baal was the supreme deity in Canaan's large pantheon of gods and ruled as the supreme storm and fertility god of the Canaanites. He reigned as king at the source of the rivers and was believed to be the father of the sons of the gods as well as the father of humankind. He was often referred to as El, the generic word for God in ancient Semitic languages. Baal was symbolized with a helmet adorned with the horns of a bull, referring to his strength and procreative power and was worshiped with continual sacrifices (see Exod. 34:13,14; 1 Sam. 31:8-10; 1 Kings 18:19; 2 Kings 21:1-7).

Baal's consort was Asherah, but the Canaanites also worshiped many other female deities. Asherah was the goddess of war to whom they dedicated their spoils of battle. She is probably the "queen of heaven" for whom the apostate Israelites made cakes and poured out drink offerings, thus provoking the anger of the Almighty and His servant Jeremiah (see Jer. 7:18; 44:17-19,25). Queen Jezebel had 400 prophets of Asherah and 450 of Baal (see 1 Kings 18:19).

The Canaanite religion was practiced openly, on every hill and under every green tree (see 1 Kings 14:23; 2 Kings 17:10; Jer. 2:20; 3:6; Ezek. 6:13). It espoused numerous magic ceremonies and fertility rites. The worship of its goddesses usually included acts of sexual perversion, so the shrines were home to both male and female cult prostitutes known as the "holy ones."[1]

Our twenty-first-century Canaan mirrors the same challenges with its many religions, cults, beliefs and immorality. Carl F. Henry, the noted historian and theologian, paints our cultural picture with clarity when he writes:

> The unraveling strands of western civilization are everywhere. Not simply at the future end of history nor even

only at the looming end of this second millennium, but already in the immediate present, modernity is being weighed in the balances. Dismay and distress follow in the wake of the rebellious despiritualization of our once vibrant civilization. Secular hedonism had nurtured the disintegration of the family and the desanctification of human existence. Spiritual dissatisfaction underlies the ready reach for a counterfeit transcendent. The inability to cope publicly with drug use and traffic is painfully apparent. On every hand one sees moral deterioration and ethical upheaval, together with attendant manifestations of melancholy and hopelessness. Amid the deteriorating cultural configurations, moral permissiveness has spawned lives scarred and marred by illegitimate sex and adultery, homosexuality and pornography.[2]

THE EDGE, THE OVERFLOW AND THE HARVEST

The position in which Israel found itself on the east of Jordan was in some respects similar to that which confronted Moses at the first crossing of Israel at the Red Sea (see Exod. 14:5-31). Joshua, however, was faced with a problem much different. With 40 years of the desert-toughened and disciplined host at his command (see Exod. 16:35; Num. 14:33,34; 32:13; Deut. 8:2-4; Josh. 5:6; 14:7,10), Joshua possessed an instrument immensely more suitable and powerful for carrying out his purposes.

The actual crossing of Jordan is set out in Joshua 3—4. There were doubtless special reasons that induced Joshua to cross Jordan at the lower fords opposite Jericho. Higher up the river an easier crossing led directly into central Palestine, a crossing that would have no fortified city such as Jericho. The city of Jericho was built in a plain 12 to 14 miles wide and stood at the mouth of the valley of Achor. Joshua's decision was probably influenced by a desire to possess a fortified base at Jericho and in the neighboring cities.

The timing of Joshua's crossing is of prophetic importance to us. Scripture expressly states that the Israelites approached the river at the time of harvest or in the early spring (see Josh. 3:15). The time of harvest was also a time when the water level would rise to flood stage and would fill the entire channel from bank to bank. As we approach the twenty-first century, signs all around us are bearing witness that the water level is rising. The water level for God's people is an ever-growing revival spirit filling our churches, cities and nations. Conversely, the ungodly culture is also experiencing a rising level of evil and wickedness.

Neil Anderson and Elmer Towns agree in their book *Rivers of Revival*:

> We are seeing many encouraging signs of the stirring of the Holy Spirit in cities and communities across the nation. There does not seem to be a single spark that may ignite a larger revival movement. Instead the Lord seems to be pouring out the showers of His Spirit on scores of individuals, local churches, Christian schools and prayer gatherings in homes, churches, around flagpoles in front of schools, in large gatherings of men in stadiums of America and in many other settings.... This is an exciting time to be alive. Not since the Day of Pentecost have we seen such phenomenal growth of the Church worldwide. Africa was less than 5 percent Christian at the turn of the century, yet is expected to be 50 percent Christian by the end of this millennium. China had only about 5 million believers when communism took control of the country. Now the estimates vary from 50 to as high as 150 million

believers. Missiologists estimate that 25,000 and 35,000 are coming to Christ daily in China.[3]

A multitude of respected voices seem to be saying the same thing: Revival waters are rising in cities and countries around the world. This could be God's strategy as we cross over these waters of revival and move into the twenty-first century as a revived and spiritually equipped Church. In his book *The Rising Revival*, Peter Wagner states:

> If we are truly in the midst of an unprecedented global prayer movement, we can expect that tangible signs of revival will be appearing and this is the case. My guess would be that more reports of revival activity have come forth in the 1990s than in the last eight decades combined. And the frequency of revival reports is accelerating dramatically year after year. Given current trends as well as words frequently being heard through intercessors and prophets, it is not unrealistic to look for a worldwide outpouring of the Holy Spirit on a magnitude never before experienced, in the very near future.[4]

Are we standing once again on the edge of a global fresh outpouring of the Holy Spirit? Are we experiencing a rising of our spiritual water level? I personally believe we are indeed standing on the threshold of mighty worldwide revivals, resulting in massive harvesting of unsaved souls into the kingdom of God. We are standing on the edge—the edge of our rivers to cross as we move into the future. Church history records solemn seasons when God seems manifestly to go before His people, expecting His people to follow. There must be no hesitation, no excuse-making mentality, no resistance to moving forward.

ONLY GOD CAN TAKE US ACROSS THE RIVER

The ordinary methods of prayer, worship and ministry will not be sufficient for this season of moving through and over these new revival rivers. We, as did Joshua and God's people in the Old Testament, must cross over *by following the manifest presence of God.* In Joshua's day, the Ark of God set out first and then the leaders followed the Ark into the waters of the Jordan as recorded in Joshua 3:14,15:

> So it was, when the people set out from their camp to cross over the Jordan, with the priests bearing the ark of the covenant before the people, and as those who bore the ark came to the Jordan, and the feet of the priests who bore the ark dipped in the edge of the water (for the Jordan overflows all its banks during the whole time of harvest).

His presence may, especially during revival seasons, lead us in most unusual ways to get us into the flood waters of the Jordan (the river of God). Stepping into a river flowing at flood stage is not the normal way to cross a river! It poses many dangers and raises many fears. We may fear that we will be swept away in the rising waters. We may fear we will lose the security of standing on the banks, but we must trust God's manifest presence. We set out. We let go. We wade into the water.

THE RIVER OF GOD DEFINED

Let me define more specifically what I mean by the river of God. It is the spiritual flow of revival caused by Holy Spirit activity in and around present truths that is at certain times effected by seasonal outpourings of God's presence. The stream or river of

God is God's work worldwide. It is the Spirit of the sovereign Lord actively manifesting His redeeming power everywhere.

God's desire is to get us from where we are

to where He is working. When God reveals

to you where He is working, that is your

invitation to join Him.

As already stated, there is global Holy Spirit activity that has provoked the Church to move into and embrace what God is doing, to let the rivers of revival refresh, reshape and refill with the power of God.

If God is the author of these many new outpourings of revival passion, then we must set out to follow Him. We must humbly put our feet into the water and cross over. God's desire is to get us from where we are to where He is working. When God reveals to you where He is working, that becomes your invitation to join Him. When God reveals His work to you, that is His timing for you to respond.

THE SYMBOLIC USE OF RIVERS

Scripture commonly uses rivers to be symbolic of God's presence or His Spirit (see Ps. 1:1-3; John 7:37-39; Rev. 22:1), but rivers can also be used for other symbolic teachings. One Hebrew word for river is *nahal* meaning a wadi or a torrent valley. Summer's dry riverbed or ravine would become a raging torrent during the rainy season. The River Jabbok (see Deut. 2:37) was such a river as were all the streams mentioned in Elijah's stories. Because these riverbeds could suddenly become raging torrents, they often came to symbolize the pride of nations (see Isa. 66:12), the strength of the invader (see Jer. 47:2) and the power of the enemy (see Ps. 124:4).[5]

The river of God is seen in the Garden of Eden (see Gen. 2:10), in Ezekiel's Temple (see Ezek. 47:1-10), in the believer (see John 7:37-39) and in the new city of God (see Rev. 22:1). All of these representations easily demonstrate the power of God's presence to bring new life and fruitfulness.

The New Testament uses the river to symbolize the salvation of God, the life or power of God and the Holy Spirit's imparting and cleansing (see John 3:5; 4:13,14; 7:37-39; 13:10; Titus 3:5). In the new city of God (see Rev. 22:1-5), the pure water does not issue from the Temple as in Ezekiel 47:12; instead it comes from the throne of God for the healing of the nations.[6]

The river of God that flows to God's people is an outpouring of His Spirit for the purpose of bringing healing to the nations, healing to our sick and dying culture. We desperately need a deep and living river of God in our sick and dying churches worldwide. We need a refreshing river for a discouraged and disconnected twenty-first-century Church. We need God's river!

MANY STREAMS, ONE RIVER

The headwaters of revival have three distinct levels of flowing water before the river level is reached—rills, brooks and streams. Rills are tiny narrow channels of water that multiply and form wider deeper channels called brooks. And brooks again merge with other brooks gaining momentum and depth that eventually become streams, which are more permanent and grow larger.

Rills, brooks and streams are the tributaries that create rivers. First the natural, then the spiritual.

Like tributaries (rills, brooks and streams) that carry water to a river and form a river system, the spiritual tributaries of revival rivers have multiple sources behind them. The God-way to create a river of Holy Spirit activity that will ultimately affect all denominations, churches, cultures, cities and nations is to allow all the tributaries to flow into and create one massive river.

Each stream is important and absolutely necessary to create a river. The more streams flowing together, the more powerful the river becomes. For streams to flow together, they must acknowledge the fact that they are not the river. And yet each stream within God's spiritual tributaries commonly believes that it is the river and that all other streams will eventually see its revelation of truth and join it, or at least embrace the truths its stream holds.

Today the Holy Spirit is certainly breaking down the walls of attitude that movements have built to separate themselves. As each stream humbles itself and, with sincerity and honesty, embraces the other streams and cross-pollinates with those streams, the river of God increases in power and depth.

JORDAN, THE RIVER OF DEATH AND LIFE

The Jordan River depression is a unique geographical formation. Formed as a result of a rift valley, it is the lowest depression on earth. Thus the name Jordan in the Hebrew, *Yarden*, aptly means "the descender." The Jordan River is the largest watercourse in Palestine; its distance of some 75 miles from Lake Huleh to the Dead Sea is more than doubled by its meandering path.

No other river has more biblical allusions and significance. In Christian hymnody and preaching, the Jordan River has often symbolized the transition of death from this life to the next. Indeed, the Jordan River also represented a death of sorts to the Hebrew children. Prophetically it represents a river we all must pass through each time we embrace revival rivers.

Revival rivers are first a river of death to self, to pride and to a religious spirit. They are a place we must pass through that brings death to our human and carnal power, our natural strength and ability to perform. Before Joshua could take the cities of Canaan, he and the people had to pass through the Jordan, which was a river of death before it could become a river of life.

Come, step into the Jordan. Every leader, every stream, every movement is invited. It may not look inviting or dignifying and may not be what you expected, but it is the first step to crossing the rivers of God. We, like Namaan of old, must be willing to dip seven times in rivers that are not necessarily our type or from our cultural context.

Why was he asked to dip seven times? Seven is God's number for wholeness. Only when we are willing to accept ALL that He has for us can we be made whole.

NAMAAN'S RESPONSE TO THE JORDAN

And Elisha sent a messenger to him, saying, "Go and wash in the Jordan seven times, and your flesh shall be restored to you, and you shall be clean" (2 Kings 5:10).

A simple message given to Namaan caused a furious response:

But Namaan became furious, and went away and said, "Indeed, I said to myself, 'He will surely come out to me, and stand and call on the name of the LORD his God, and wave his hand over the place, and heal the leprosy'" (2 Kings 5:11).

His thinking was: *Couldn't I dip myself in the Abanah or Pharpar Rivers, the rivers of Damascus? Aren't they better than all the rivers in Israel?* We too may be challenged to dip into rivers that are not of our making and not of our choosing. Yet they are rivers that God has chosen to bring restoration and life to us.

What was it that finally convinced Namaan to dip in the muddy Jordan, the river he disliked by reputation and by natural understanding? Desperation and a willingness to be humbled. Yes, a little swallowing of his military self-will and pompous attitude. A lesser leader encouraged him by saying in effect, "If the prophet had told you to do something hard, impossible, unbearable, wouldn't you have done it? So why not do it when all he says to you is 'Wash, and be clean'?" This reasoning caused the great Namaan to humble himself enough to go down and dip seven times in the muddy, dirty, undesirable Jordan. Not once. Not twice. Seven times. He was asked to dip in the Jordan until He was thoroughly saturated by the Jordan River.

Every river of revival has its good and bad, its human and divine. This mixture causes some to respond like Namaan with a "No, not that river. How could God bless that river with all its obvious flaws, human carnality and shallow doctrine? It doesn't make sense." But the ways of the Spirit are not always logical or rational. Nevertheless, we must drink deeply from all rivers sent by the Holy Spirit.

In the words of Joshua 3:1: "And came to the Jordan...and lodged there before they crossed over." We must lodge at the river.

LODGING AT THE RIVER

Revival necessitates two steps: (1) lodging at the river and (2) crossing over. Some might take the first step and never move to the second, so enthralled and satisfied with the lodging that they

have no desire for the crossing. Others will desire only the crossing of the river, never allowing any time to lodge at the river. We
must do both. This is not just revival wisdom—it is spiritually
healthy—a matter of life or death.

The word lodge used in Joshua 3:1 means to stop and stay
for a length of time, to lie down and stay still, to patiently
remain and tarry. When the Holy Spirit is doing something new
and fresh, the greatest need is to lodge. The greatest gift during
revival times is not necessarily the gift of leadership, but the gift of
fellowship. Knowing we do not have all the answers creates a holy
desperation which is found by those who lodge at the river and are
willing to keep dipping into the new, sometimes uncomfortable,
thing that God is asking them to experience.

Whether we're in full-time church ministry as a pastor, elder or
missionary or a secular ministry such as a carpenter, electrician or
sales person, we all need to lodge at the river. We need to camp out
with God. We need to take time, be patient, wait on God through
prayer, fasting, worship, cleansing through repentance and hearing
God's Word with an open heart. As the spiritual flow of the Holy
Spirit increases in our midst, we will have the opportunity to drink
from that river, receiving newness of spirit, soul and body. We must
develop a personal love and commitment to drink deeply of revival
rivers as God allows them to flow near us and through us.

LODGING: GOD'S CURE FOR
SPIRITUAL DROUGHT

Spiritually dry souls in desert places are prime candidates for the
refreshing river of God. A person, family, church or group of
churches may be in a spiritual drought, in desperate need of a
genuine spiritual awaking, in need of the river of God. Perhaps
you can identify:

My vitality was turned into the drought of summer (Ps. 32:4).

My soul thirsts for You; my flesh longs for You in a dry and thirsty land where there is no water (Ps. 63:1).

The word "drought" means a continuous dry wind that blows rain clouds away, scorching the ground; a restraint of refreshing rain for long periods of time, an extended dryness in the heat of summer. "Dry," "thirsty," "rainless" and "hardened" are words that may describe your soul or your church's soul. In the natural, when a region has had a long drought, the ground becomes so hardened that the first rains will not penetrate it. Instead the first downpour can result in flash floods as the hardened ground resists the water. Several rains are needed to soften the ground. The first gentle rains begin to soften the ground slowly. Then, as additional rains come, penetrating rains, the ground softens more and more, accepting more of the water instead of cascading it off. Finally the absorbing rains begin to fall, soaking deeply into the ground, readying it for the seed to be planted and to produce fruit.

So it is with dry souls and dry churches. We need softening rains, penetrating rains and absorbing rains. The Word of God promises refreshing water to those who are in a dry and thirsty place:

He opened the rock, and water gushed out; it ran in the dry places like a river (Ps. 105:41).

He turns a wilderness into pools of water, and dry land into watersprings (Ps. 107:35).

For I will pour water on him who is thirsty, and floods on the dry ground; I will pour My Spirit on your descendants, and My blessing on your offspring (Isa. 44:3; see also Isa. 32:1,2; 41:17,18; Matt. 12:43).

Our responsibility is to stop, lodge or drink deeply of the rivers of God (see Jer. 31:12). Lodging may sound like a trivial point to enlarge upon, but I see it as one of the foundational steps to entering into revival rivers in the twenty-first century. We must not only come to the edge (see Josh. 3:15), but we must also wade out into the waters God has made available to us and drink deeply and personally of that water. To drink means to absorb, consume, take in. Drinking speaks of openness (see Deut. 11:11; Jer. 31:12; John 4:14, 7:37-39; Eph. 5:18).

Prepare your heart, mind and spirit with expectation and faith to receive (see 2 Kings 3:16,17). Dig out a place for the Holy Spirit to fill up. Open your hands. Open your spirit. Drink. Absorb. Let the breath of God's Spirit breathe new life into you (see John 20:22) and receive power from on high for the crossing (see Acts 1:8).

Over and Over Again
By Mark Strauss

There is a fountain
That I have found in You,
Only You, Lord.
You are a wellspring
That I keep drinking from,
Yet I need more.
Here I am, asking for more again.

Come, Jesus, fill me again,
Over and over again.

Come, Spirit, like gentle wind,
Over and over again.
Wave after wave, like an endless ocean;
Jesus, I pray with intense devotion.
Keep filling me deep within,
Over and over again.

There is a thirsting
That You have birthed in me for Your Spirit,
A holy hunger,
A heart that longs for more.
Come and fill it.
Here I am, asking for more again.[7]

PERSONAL APPLICATION

1. As we are seeing concurrent levels of revival and evil waters rising, we must be willing to tear down the Baals that attempt to crowd out the Lord of the Harvest. What Baals do you need to reckon with in order to maintain a soul-winning focus?
2. Most of us have blindsighted areas where we are sure that our doctrines and denominations are the river rather than tributaries that contribute to the river. Will you ask the Holy Spirit to expose any veiled areas of pride or rigidity in you?
3. Can you relate to Naaman? What outrageous ideas has God asked you to accept that you refuse to dip into as part of God's solution for taking you to the Promised Land?
4. Before any of us can bring the refreshing waters of revival to others, we must be refreshed ourselves. Are

you lodging in God's presence? If not, could it be that
you need to bring your self-effort into the Jordan?

Notes

1. J. A. Thompson, *Handbook of Life in Bible Times* (Downers Grove, IL:
   InterVarsity Press, 1986), pp. 318-320.
2. Carl F. Henry, *Gods of This Age or God of the Ages* (Nashville: Broadman
   Holman Publishers, 1992), p. 2.
3. Neil Anderson and Elmer Towns, *Rivers of Revival* (Ventura, CA: Renew
   Books, 1997), pp. 12, 15.
4. C. Peter Wagner and Pablo Deiros, *The Rising Revival* (Ventura, CA: Renew
   Books, 1998), p. 8.
5. J. D. Douglas, *The New Bible Dictionary* (Grand Rapids: Wm. B. Eerdman's
   Publishing Company, 1974), p. 1098.
6. Frank E. Gaebelein, *Expositor's Bible Commentary, New International Version,
   Volume 2* (Grand Rapids: Zondervan, 1992), p. 599.
7. Mark Strauss, "Over and Over Again," City Bible Music, 1997. Used with
   permission.

CHAPTER 3

PREPARATION
FOR THE CROSSING

*They set out from Acacia Grove and came to the
Jordan, he and all the children of Israel, and lodged
there before they crossed over.*

JOSHUA 3:1

As we embrace our Jordan, the rivers of God's presence, and prepare for this generation, we move into our future and grasp our destiny. The cities before us are tightly shut up to heaven, sealed by evil influences and invisible powers. These places are our inheritance, our challenge, our future. But we need a fresh anointing of God's Holy Spirit, a fresh, supernatural, city-reaching power to secure that inheritance.

Revivals come to first transform the Church and then transform the unsaved world. God must come and be received by His own people before He can be proclaimed to the unsaved. Revival rivers were never meant to be captured by and owned by the Church only. Rivers of revival are to flow out from the house of

God into every valley, wilderness, desert and walled city. We, as Joshua did, must come to the edge of each revival river and prepare ourselves to step into the river, to cross over the river, taking with us new power, new truths, new faith and new vision.

THE ACACIA GROVE, A BOOT CAMP FOR THE CROSSING

The preparation for embracing new movings of God's Holy Spirit and then assimilating those outpourings into our lives, ministries and churches starts with cleansing. Joshua 3:1 says, "and they set out from Acacia Grove and came to the Jordan." The Acacia Grove experience is foundational to moving to the edge of the river and stepping in to cross over it.

The very core of our Christian living must

be examined, cleansed and changed if we

are to cross the rivers of God and touch

entire cities for Christ.

Acacia wood was named for its durability. In the Hebrew, the word "acacia" means nondecaying, durable, and was sometimes translated "incorruptible wood" in the Septuagint. The Acacia Grove experience is a fresh and life-changing encounter with true biblical holiness. Holiness and the twenty-first-century, modern-day culture are destined to clash in every way possible.

The shifts that have occurred in today's value system have been megashifts. The humanistic, syncretistic philosophy of our world culture has eroded all moral value systems. We now face a new culture, a new Canaan to enter, a culture separated from God and His Word.

If the Acacia Grove experience is ignored, detoured around or found to be distasteful to those seeking revival, then revival will be a mixture of flesh and spirit, shallow and short lived. The very core of our Christian living must be examined, cleansed and changed if we are to cross the rivers of God and touch entire cities for Christ. A stop at Acacia is not optional!

HOLINESS, THE FRUIT OF THE ACACIA GROVE

Holiness is one of the most frequent descriptive terms used of God. The Lord is called "the Holy One" more than 30 times in Isaiah alone. The word "holy" occurs more than 600 times in the Bible, and one entire book, Leviticus, is devoted to the subject of holiness. As we can see from the following Scriptures, God places a high premium on holiness and demands personal and corporate holiness from His people.

Pursue peace with all men, and *holiness*, without which no one will see the Lord (Heb. 12:14, italics added).

Therefore, having these promises, beloved, let us *cleanse ourselves* from all filthiness of the flesh and spirit, perfecting *holiness* in the fear of God (2 Cor. 7:1, italics added).

But as He who called you is *holy*, you also be *holy* in all your conduct, because it is written, "Be holy, for I am holy" (1 Pet. 1:15,16, italics added).

I speak in human terms because of the weakness of your flesh. For just as you presented your members as slaves of uncleanness, and of lawlessness leading to more lawlessness, so now present your members as slaves of righteousness for holiness (Rom. 6:19).

The word "holiness" causes many different responses and reactions in today's Church. People may conjure up bad memories of hellfire and brimstone messages, hammering on hairstyles, modern make-up, dress styles and entertainment taboos. True holiness, however, is God's idea and therefore must be attainable and spiritually satisfying to all believers who seek God.

The primary meaning of holy is "separate." It comes from an ancient word that means to cut or separate. In contemporary language, we would use the phrase "to cut apart" or "a cut above." *Strong's Concordance* defines holy as "morally blameless."[1] *Vine's Expository Dictionary* states, "Holiness is separated to God from sin with conduct befitting one so separated."[2] A. W. Pink says, "Holiness consists of that internal change or renovation of our souls whereby our minds, affections and wills are brought into harmony with God."[3]

The Hebrew verb *qadash* is translated in various ways throughout the Old Testament: to dedicate, hallow, consecrate, sanctify, set apart, keep holy, make holy and to purify. Opposite verbs would be to pollute, mix, compromise, profane, join with evil, make a covenant with evil, desecrate, spot or blemish, stain or make common. Again, the basic biblical concept and meaning of holiness is a separation. Just a glance at *Strong's Concordance* under the word "holy" reminds us of how many things were and still are called holy:

holy law	holy covenant	holy of holies
holy prophets	holy brethren	holy women

holy conduct	holy priests	holy altar
holy incense	holy feasts	holy Scriptures
holy name	holy angels	holy place
holy apostles	holy hands	holy gift
holy children	holy Sabbath	holy congregation
holy city	holy father	Holy Spirit
holy mountain	holy child	holy calling
holy people	holy kiss	holy nation

Moving toward a river of God's power and presence, whether it be a national revival river or the river of God that we encounter every Sunday when we come together, we must visit the Acacia Grove for cleansing, purifying and releasing. Second Corinthians 7:1 confirms this: "Therefore, having these promises, beloved, let us cleanse ourselves from all filthiness of the flesh and spirit, perfecting holiness in the fear of God." (See also Lev. 11:44; 1 Sam. 16:5; John 17:16,17; 2 Tim. 2:2; Heb. 2:11.)

THE COLLISION BETWEEN HOLINESS AND CULTURE

Holiness is in direct confrontation with a culture gone astray. We are ruled by the notion that life somehow gives us the right to have every whim and desire fulfilled. Our nation, and seemingly most nations, is driven by the pursuit of pleasures, self-fulfillment, sexual perversions and more. We live in a world that believes in exhausting itself on the mistaken notion that physical pleasures produce happiness. Our nation dismisses the idea of the wrath of God as a product of puritan prudishness. Moral absolutes are nothing more than psychological hang-ups to be healed. We desperately need a long stop at the Acacia Grove, returning to the biblical concepts of holiness, purity and godly standards.

Chuck Colson agrees:

> It strikes me that the prevalent characteristic of our culture today is rampant narcissism, materialism and hedonism. Our culture passes itself off as Christian with 50 million Americans, according to George Gallup, claiming to be born again. But it is dominated almost entirely by relativism. The do-your-own-thing mind-set has liberated us from the absolute structure of faith and belief and set us adrift in a sea of nothingness.[4]

We are challenged but not discouraged to be living in such a culture, for all around us are signs of God desiring to bring a revival of truth, right thinking, godly values, and a Church victorious and conquering. As we pursue holiness, let us with knowledge lay aside those philosophies that may hinder our pursuit.

> Therefore we also, since we are surrounded by so great a cloud of witnesses, let us lay aside every weight, and the sin which so easily ensnares us, and let us run with endurance the race that is set before us, looking unto Jesus, the author and finisher of our faith, who for the joy that was set before Him endured the cross, despising the shame, and has sat down at the right hand of the throne of God (Heb. 12:1,2).

EXPOSING MODERN-DAY HINDRANCES

At the Acacia Grove, cop-out practices and philosophies that have subtly and insidiously infiltrated the Church culture with too much religion and too little relationship are exposed and reckoned with. The following are just a few that keep us from stepping into our Jordan of destiny.

- **Legalism:** Legalism hinders believers by squeezing every decision into a strict and often overly literalistic interpretation of the Scriptures (or church tradition). For a legalist, rules and regulations are seen as directives to be meticulously followed, rather than guidelines or principles to be applied with wisdom and insight in varying circumstances. In its worst form, legalism assumes that salvation itself can be earned by the work of following God's laws—a mockery of the New Testament teaching on the helplessness of humans to do works pleasing to God apart from the mercy and grace of God through Jesus Christ.
- **Libertarianism:** Libertarianism begins with a person freely creating his or her own standards and values, expressing them in words and action, without having to be burdened by timeless principles, maxims or rules; one must rely on self alone for the correct ethical course. This is not a new philosophy; it can be seen as the understanding by which Israel brought disaster upon itself, everyone doing "what was right in his own eyes" (Judg. 17:6; see Prov. 12:15).
- **Existentialism:** Like libertarianism, existentialism rejects what it regards as abstract moral truths given by God or gods in favor of the concrete existence of humans and whatever values or ethics they have chosen. Existentialism emphasizes that in each present moment, we as individuals are totally free and must by the force of will create our own meaning. And to make authentic choices, we cannot rely on our reason, which

leads us only to disagreements and paradoxes, but instead to our inner (irrational) consciousness. Jean-Paul Sartre, the most famous proponent of existentialism, said, "Man is condemned to freedom." This total freedom creates anxiety: about the realization of absolute nonexistence after death; about no God and no judgment; and about the realization that Hitler's choice for terror and the "final solution" was no more or less legitimate than Saint Francis's choice for goodness and peace! Existentialists rely on their gut feelings rather than absolute truth. They rely on themselves rather than God. Existentialism places the priority on the emotional rather than reason, asking, How can it be wrong if it feels so right?

- **Situation Ethics:** The situation ethicist enters every decision-making situation with the assumption that the "situation" heavily influences ethical decisions and can even overturn existing morality. The highest value for situationists is usually described as "love." If a person embraces this philosophy, biblical holiness is impossible because true holiness begins with the absolute Word of God.
- **Pragmatism:** Pragmatism says that whatever brings satisfaction and whatever works is right and good. Pragmatism expresses one of the main inspirations of American culture and of the techno-scientific era. To a pragmatist, the end justifies the means.
- **Relativism:** Relativism takes many forms—the main idea is that "what's true or right for you may or may not be what's true or right for me." Relativism can be expressed as cultural relativism, ethical relativism and relativism of personal worlds. In relativism there are no objective standards of truth or justice—everything is relative.

• **Humanism:** Secular humanism dethrones God as the center of life and enshrines humanity instead. The tenets of humanism are atheism, evolution, amorality, autonomous man and a socialist, one worldview. Regarding amorality, the Humanist Manifesto says, "In the area of sexuality we believe that intolerant attitudes are often cultivated by orthodox religions which unduly repress sexual conduct. The right to birth control, abortion and divorce should be recognized. Neither do we wish to prohibit sexual behavior between consenting adults."

The following is a summary of our culture's moral beliefs:

• There are no God-given moral laws.
• There are no objective moral laws.
• There are no timeless moral laws.
• There are no laws against laws.
• There are no restraints to pleasures.
• There are no restrictions to individuals' choices.
• There are no absolutes or principles to live by.

When you put biblical holiness, which is founded upon biblical absolutes, up against a tidal wave of nonbiblical philosophies, you feel the overwhelming pressure of encouraging a livable holiness.

As a pastor of a multigenerational, multiethnic church in a fairly large city, I am—as we all are—faced with every kind of sinful enticement. Our congregation is conservative about moral standards and biblical convictions regarding entertainment and overall living. We preach and teach against moral looseness, sinful behavior and habits, and take a clear stand against premarital sex, adultery and any other clear moral sin. Our pastors, counselors, lay pastors, small group leaders, youth leaders and college leaders all have some form of accountability and a clear standard for living as leaders. Yet with all of this, it is absolutely amazing how much sin, sinful behavior, unbroken sinful lifestyle patterns and unconfessed moral failure exists at some level in our congregation.

I believe that every church battles with these same laws of degeneration. Some pastors, leaders, bishops and elders may become discouraged and overwhelmed with the struggle of leading a congregation into biblical holiness. This is exactly why we must always journey to our Acacia Grove, our place of touching the holiness of God, receiving the newness of life that conquers the old.

Scripture says that we pastors lead holy people—some with foolish and sinful behaviors. At all times, our holiness is found in our position in Christ first.

The Bible does call the believer a saint, a word that simply means holy one. We might stumble over this, but the Scripture says that we pastors lead holy people—some with foolish and sinful behaviors. At all times, our holiness is found in our position in Christ first. We must claim Christ's perfection as we deal with our imperfections and expect a continual and gradual work of sanctification.

In one of our services, I instructed the congregation to write down privately a sin or sins that were besetting sins: lifestyles, habit patterns, life weaknesses. We then spent time on our knees confessing, repenting and asking God for cleansing, deliverance and freedom. After our time of repentance, I then asked the church to bring these pieces of paper forward and deposit them in two large trash cans at the altar. We experienced a very unusual sense of God's grace and power as people placed their sins in the trash can. I then had the pieces of paper burned, collected the ashes and put them into a bottle that sits on my desk. You may think this is strange, but it is a reminder to me that our congregation has given up these ashes in order to receive the beauty of the Lord (see Isa. 61:1-4). This congregation, with all our defects and faults, is claiming God's miracle-working grace to take the best or worst of our sins and turn them into ashes, giving us His beauty.

ACACIA GROVE PRINCIPLES

There are no set formulas for livable holiness, but there are clear biblical principles to follow. The following are just a few of the principles that come from the Acacia Grove:

- Everything is permissible for me but everything is not beneficial (see 1 Cor. 6:12).
- Everything is permissible for me, but I will not be mastered by anything. I will not allow anything to bring me under its power (see 1 Cor. 6:12).
- If something is permissible but hurts other people, I will refrain (see 1 Cor. 8:13).
- In everything I do, I will purpose to bring glory to God (see 1 Cor. 10:31).
- I will keep my thoughts lined up with the Word of God.

My thoughts are as important as my actions (see 1 Sam. 16:7; Ps. 139:1-4; Prov. 23:7; Phil. 4:8).
- I will transform my habits into godly disciplines for living (see Rom. 6:19; 12:1,2; 2 Tim. 3:16).

We concur that holiness is the believer's separation from the cares, lusts and carnal culture of the world around us in response to God's call to be a holy people who are set apart unto God. This holy calling is a sovereign act of God, whereas the perfecting of holiness is an ongoing, everyday, gradual, continual responsibility of every believer and every church. As we desire to enter into the river of God's presence and purpose continually, we make a commitment to holiness—we choose the Acacia Grove.

Your testimonies are very sure; holiness adorns Your house, O LORD, forever (Ps. 93:5).

I Cry Holy
By Mark Strauss

I see Your throne lifted high;
Angels bow down giving glory.
I hear a multitude cry:
"Holy, holy!"

Lord by Your grace I draw near;
I join this heavenly chorus,
Echoing that which I hear:
"Holy, holy, holy, Lord!"

I cry, "Holy, holy!"
You're the spotless Lamb,

The sinless Son of Man.
I cry, "Holy, holy!"
You have paid the price with Your sacrifice.
In You I stand complete
To worship at Your feet.
I cry, "Holy, holy, Lord!"[5]

PERSONAL APPLICATION

1. On a scale of 1 to 10, how important is holiness to you? Does your life reflect that kind of holiness?
2. Christians sometimes sacrifice loving relationship for rules that elevate the tree of the knowledge of good and evil. When that happens, we bring judgment (legalism) rather than grace to others. Can you identify any modern-day philosophies and practices that have subtly influenced your thinking, causing you to compromise God's Word?
3. Set aside a moment to list your besetting sins (if you think you don't have any, consider listing pride). Burn the list. Now ask God to bring something good out of your ashes.
4. Reread the Acacia Grove principles. Which ones do you need to realign with before stepping into your river of destiny?

Notes
1. *Strong's Exhaustive Concordance of the Bible* (New York: Abingdon Press, 1890), p. 7.
2. W. E. Vine, *Vine's Expository Dictionary of New Testament Words* (London: Oliphants, 1957), p. 2251.

3. A. W. Pink, *The Doctrine of Sanctification* (Evangel, PA: Bible Truth Depot, 1955), p. 7.
4. Chuck Colson, source unknown.
5. Mark Strauss, "I Cry Holy," City Bible Music, 1997. Used with permission.

CHAPTER 4

RIVERS OF
REVIVAL IN THE
TWENTY-FIRST CENTURY

*When you have come to the edge of the water of the
Jordan, you shall stand in the Jordan.*

JOSHUA 3:8

The crossing of rivers for the twenty-first-century Church is the
embracing of present Holy Spirit rivers that could be classified
revival rivers. Revival rivers have been present in most generations
and the Church has always had the choice of moving into the
river, bypassing the river, ignoring the river or reacting to the
river. When a generation reacts to or misses the river of God, it may
be a Judges 2:10 generation: "Another generation arose after them
who did not know the LORD, nor the work which He had done for
Israel." Reverend Bevon Jones states, "Never let a generation grow
up without that knowledge of divine things which may contain
the germ of national revival in years to come."[1]

Portraits of Revivals Past

Every generation has the potential to experience a generation gap or a revival gap. We face it today as did previous generations—the cycle of change and decay, of reformation and apostasy. To break in upon this cycle of decline, God sends revivals, rivers of His Holy Spirit to awaken and revive His people.

Each generation has had its chosen leaders, reformers and revivalists who were used to turn the Church toward the river of revival. In the dark days of the twelfth century, there was Frances of Assisi in his brown monk's robe who used words like fire to pierce the heart. In the fourteenth century, Savanarola, a man steeped in the Scriptures and Holy Spirit, called his generation to repentance. He was a fasting, praying, prophetic preacher who spoke with the fire power of the Holy Spirit, affecting his generation. The reformer Martin Luther (1483-1546) touched his generation with his powerful messages and leadership in a reformation that changed the course of history. Martin Luther embraced the river of God, crossed through the river and reached his generation with revival-reformation truths. By 1517, Luther gave us the basic framework of present Protestant theology. He had been convinced of three basic points:

- A man is justified by faith alone and not by works.
- Each believer has access to God directly apart from any human intermediaries.
- The Bible is the supreme source of authority for both faith and life.

God is deeply committed to visit each and every generation with His divine presence and power. Space does not allow us to speak of John and Charles Wesley, George Whitfield, Ludwig von Zinzendorf, John Calvin, Charles Finney, Jonathan Edwards, D. L. Moody and the Great Awakenings in our own nation. Revival rivers have always been available—disguised, unlikely, outside our camp—but always there. The 1905-1906 Awakening rolled like a tidal wave through our nation and around the world. Pentecostal denominations find their beginnings in this turn-of-the-century revival. Now again, today, we are faced with many different rivers of revival. Some may be only rills, brooks or small streams. Others may be true rivers of Holy Spirit power and presence.

PORTRAITS OF REVIVALS PRESENT

The people and places that have taken on national and international interest are controversial to many, a blessing to thousands and possibly another potential river of revival for the Church. These are people such as Rodney Howard-Browne of South Africa who arrived in the United States in 1987 and made an impact in many parts of our nation as well as in the Philippines, Singapore, Russia and Africa. People have rejected and attacked Rodney for the Laughing Revival just as passionately as others have passionately received him.

John and Carol Arnott of Toronto, Canada, invited Randy Clark for revival meetings beginning January 20, 1994—meetings which continue to this day. The Toronto Blessing has touched multiplied thousands with a new love for God, the Holy Spirit and the simplicity of receiving more of Jesus. The Arnotts, a humble couple, joyfully anointed, claim that this revival is easy to receive. "Everybody can catch it if they will soak in it. It is transferable and highly contagious." Leaders from many nations arrived in Toronto to drink from the waters of this revival: Switzerland, Germany, France, Sweden, Norway, England,

Scotland and more, as well as most major cities in the United States and Canada. All were affected by this unusual outburst of God's river.

Again, many thousands were blessed, churches transformed, pastors by the thousands testified to a revived heart for God and His Holy Spirit. Yet some were offended and confused, blatantly rejecting and calling this river a counterfeit revival. Hank Hanegraaf, in his book *Counterfeit Revival*, refers to several current rivers of revival. He begins his evaluation with strong accusations that these revivals are more similar to cults than to works of God:

What can Heaven's Gate, Waco and Jonestown have in common with a church near you?

As incredible as it may seem, the principles used by leaders of cults are today employed in literally thousands of churches worldwide. Tactics once relegated to the ashrams of cults are now replicated at the altars of churches—as Christians worldwide ape the practices of pagan spirituality:

- Pensacola, Florida—In the emotionally charged atmosphere of the 10 o'clock Sunday morning worship of an Assemblies of God church, a woman works herself into an *altered state of consciousness* as she jerks her head violently from side to side for more than two and one half hours.
- Oklahoma City, Oklahoma—Benny Hinn Healing Crusade—Ella Peppard dies from complications suffered after someone who succumbs to the power of *peer pressure* is "slain in the spirit" on top of her.
- London, England—Holy Trinity Brompton—An Anglican vicar *exploits the expectations* of parishioners to such an

extent that they become "drunk in the Spirit." Designated drivers and taxicab services are recommended for those too spiritually inebriated to leave on their own.
• Toronto, Canada—Vineyard Christian Fellowship—A pastor employing the *subtle power of suggestion* manipulates a crowd into acting "like lions, oxen, eagles, and even warriors." Though deeply frightened, they are duped into believing their experiences are divine rather than demonic.

Socio-psychological manipulation tactics such as Altered states of consciousness, Peer pressure, Exploitation of expectations, and Subtle suggestions (A-P-E-S) are so powerful they can cause human beings to "behave like beasts or idiots and be proud of it." No one is immune—once an epidemic of hysteria is in full force, it can make black appear white, obscure realities, enshrine absurdities, and cause people to die with purple shrouds over their corpses.[2]

Hank Hanegraaf's evaluation may be an extreme reaction to rivers of revival, but it is part of mainstream Christianity's thinking. Some of his concerns are valid; some of his conclusions could be a mixture of fear and carnal reaction. Whether you feel as strongly as Hank Hanegraaf or only have doubts and questions as to the validity of these revivals, you are still faced with their existence.

Nevertheless, the Toronto Blessing has conservatively affected more than 2,000 churches in England alone, the Holy Trinity Brampton Church being a main hot spot in London. Ken and Lois Gott of Sunderland, England, visited Toronto and received a life-changing touch of the Holy Spirit. Upon returning home to Sunderland, they set out on a three-year, every-night revival that touched thousands of laypeople as well as thousands of pastors.

Another modern-day river of revival is Brownsville Assembly of God in Brownsville, Florida. On Father's Day, June 18, 1995, evangelist Steve Hill was invited to speak that Sunday only at Brownsville Assembly. Revival broke out. Now, almost four years later, the meetings continue with thousands flying, busing and driving from all around the world. Thousands have answered the salvation altar call, and multiplied thousands have rededicated their lives. Pastors have been melted by the presence of God. A clear and forceful message on holiness and cleansing is woven into each sermon with a simple biblical salvation call. Almost 2 million have passed through the doors of Brownsville Assembly.[3]

The book *Revival* by John Arnott, Malcolm McDow and Alvin Reid records the stories of current revival rivers on college campuses. Revival is spreading to multiplied college and university campuses with countless reports of repentance, reconciliation, restored relationships and thousands of salvations and prodigals returning to the Lord. Revival rivers are flowing across campuses—Indiana Wesleyan College in Marion, Indiana; Bethel College in Mishawaka, Indiana; Judson College in Elgin, Illinois; George Fox College in Newberg, Oregon; Multnomah Bible College in Portland, Oregon; Louisiana Tech University in Rustin, Louisiana; Illinois Baptist College in Galesburg, Illinois; Spring Arbor College in Spring Arbor, Michigan; Biola University in Los Angeles, California, and dozens of others.[4]

The reports of revival are varied and numerous, another revival to embrace, another river to cross.

Revival rivers are flowing in all parts of the world. One hot spot is Argentina. Peter Wagner says, "Argentina must be considered among the chief headwaters of the rivers of revival that God is now sending into many parts of the world. Any expectation is that this influence will increase significantly in the days to come. Argentina is an ordinary nation that has come under an extraordinary outpouring of the grace of God."[5]

Argentina has been in revival for more than 15 years. Usually revivals only last 3 years, maybe 10 years, some as long as 30 years (the Second Great Awakening lasted from 1800 to 1830). In Argentina the revival is prayer-centered, emphasizing holiness, evangelism and the reaching of entire cities with the gospel. Men such as Carlos Annacondia, Pablo Battori, Omar Cabrera, Claudio Freidzon, Edward Lorenzo and Ed Silvoso are all busy being used of God to light fires in Argentina.

I have had an opportunity to meet and be with all of these men, some in Argentina and some in our own church. They are men of integrity, men of prayer and men with a passion for revival. The Argentina stream has poured into our nation through the Toronto and Brownsville Revivals, both of which had their beginnings from those influenced by the Argentina Revival.

TESTING THE WATERS OF REVIVAL

As Joshua came to the edge of the waters of the Jordan, so the Church comes to the edge of revival rivers. These rivers are to be crossed. We are to dip our feet into the waters and then cross through the river, allowing the river to soak us, refresh us and add to us.

And when we come to the edge of these different streams, we should ask ourselves some pertinent questions: Is this revival river authentic? Does it have authentic biblical elements that we can spiritually discern? Does it have the ingredients of revival longevity—principles, truths and leaders of integrity? If I cross this river, will the people of God receive from it and will we be able to handle it? What might I find in the river if I have eyes to see beyond the flowing waters, beyond the noise of the current, beyond the refreshing we will enjoy in the river?

Revival rivers must touch the marketplace

as much as they touch the heavenlies.

All of the different revival rivers have some truths to deposit into our churches so that we move from visitation to habitation. God's desire is that the river flows into His house, the Church. Jesus moved from the countryside, from the streets, into a house (see Mark 2:1), and the house was full of people because Jesus was in the house. The revival rivers must move from conferences to churches, from great convention services to the weekly gatherings of God's people, from spiritual experiences to spiritual growth and maturity evidenced in both congregational life and family life. Revival rivers must touch the marketplace as much as they touch the heavenlies.

PRESERVING THE STONES WITHOUT POLLUTING THE RIVER

How do we capture the Holy Spirit truths from each of these revival rivers without damaging our churches, our families and our ministries? Toronto was a humbling and spiritually enlarging experience for me and ultimately for our church. But I need to add that we didn't become a Toronto church, nor did our church resemble the Toronto Revival. We did have repentance, weeping and new tenderness toward the Holy Spirit. People were on the floor at times, but we still maintained our God-given river, our basic discernible distinctives that we have built upon for many decades.

When we dip into authentic revival rivers, I believe these spiritual experiences, truths or emphases should be assimilated into the river that God has already given each church. Trouble arises when we believe the unique model of another revival church or movement with a specific and unique revival river should become our new model.

Our particular local church is built upon what we discern to be biblical values or distinctives. For more than four decades these distinctives have been proven to build healthy local churches with a continual flowing river of God. Seasonal outpourings of God's Spirit, like seasonal rains, have enlarged or added to our river, but we do have a year-round river.

Each revival river I have mentioned, and several I haven't, has had some influence on our river because we journeyed to the edge of each river, dipped into the river, found some memorial stones, stones of truth that we could carry out of that river and deposit into our river. Even in so doing, we maintained our values and distinctives.

Values and beliefs are critical dimensions in church effectiveness because they serve as the basis for direction and action. According to management expert Philip Selznick, "The formation of an institution is marked by the making of value commitments and the institutional leader is primarily an expert in the promotion and protection of values."

You might be asking, "What are your values and distinctives?" Let me explain them simply and forthrightly.

WITHOUT VISION VALUES, OUR PURPOSE WILL PERISH

Our vision is built upon our values. Vision provides the church with clear direction, bringing the future into focus and motivating all to become involved. Our vision is to be an effective instrument of God by raising up a local church in our region that will be restored to biblical pattern and power, which then becomes an instrument for Kingdom purposes, a harvesting church that reaches and keeps the harvest. Our vision simply stated is:

Exalting the Lord by dynamic, Holy Spirit-inspired worship, praise and prayer, giving our time, talents and gifts as an offering to the Lord.

Equipping the saints to fulfill their destiny through godly vision, biblical teaching and pastoral ministries, bringing believers to maturity in Christ and effective ministry, resulting in a restored triumphant church.

Extending the kingdom of God through the church to our city, our nation and the world through aggressive evangelism, training leaders, planting churches and sending missionaries and missions teams.

Vision is that which a congregation perceives by the Holy Spirit as pertaining to God's purpose for them, thereby creating spiritual momentum, resulting in spiritual advancement and maintained through spiritual warfare. Our *vision values* reflect our belief system, our core convictions and our building stones to build healthy churches with year-round spiritual rivers flowing strongly. We hold in high regard these vision values. Without these values the vision would be a dead letter, resulting in institutionalism. These values breathe life into the vision and sustain the quality of the vision. The following are the vision values we embrace.

VISION VALUES

Value God's Word. We believe that the Bible is God's inspired Word, the authoritative and trustworthy rule of faith and practice for all Christians.

Value God's Manifested Presence. To enjoy God's felt/realized presence is our passion as a church. We believe there is a presence of God available to God's people as they follow the pattern of worship seen in the Psalms (see Ps. 22:3).

Value Holy Spirit Activity. Both in our personal and corporate life as believers, we welcome the moving of the Holy Spirit. The baptism of the Holy Spirit and the gifts of the Holy Spirit are part of our basic belief system.

Value the Family. We express this commitment in our strong emphasis on family in preaching, teaching, available counseling, home-school programs and a K-12 Christian school.

Value Dynamic Spontaneous Praise and Worship. The believer's response to God's presence may be seen in energetic worship with clapping, lifting hands and singing spontaneous unrehearsed songs unto the Lord.

Value the Principle of Unity. Not conformity but unity of spirit and principle. Unity may express itself in a variety of ways but still maintain the same principles and convictions so as to flow together in accomplishing vision.

Value the Holiness of God. Holiness is not legalism that is measured by outward appearance, but a true cleansing of the believer by the power of the Holy Spirit which is evidenced in Christian character and conduct. The fruit is easily born forth.

Value Fervent Prayer Intercession. We believe that intercession is the call of every believer. Therefore, the voice of prayer is heard as we pray out loud together in our opening service prayer times. This principle of prayer is believed to be the motor or powerhouse to our church life. Individual praying and fasting and prayer for the whole church is a continual and primary emphasis.

Value Reaching the Lost. We believe every believer is called to reach those individuals who do not have a personal relationship with Jesus Christ. We are committed to remain aggressive in reaching our entire city with the message of the gospel.

Value Excellence. We believe God deserves the best we have to offer; therefore, we seek to maintain a high quality of excellence in everything connected to the work of God.

Value Relationships. Our goal is to *love one another*, and we endeavor to make this goal practical through small groups called City Cells. Every believer is encouraged to develop deeper relationships with other believers that result in encouragement and accountability. This happens as we devote these times to both City Life (building and strengthening each other) and City Reach (reaching our community) emphasis.

Value Integrity. There is no substitute for a lack in character. We hold this value in highest esteem and filter all other values through this one. Uprightness, trustworthiness and transparency are our best foundation stones.

Value the Kingdom of God. We desire to positively influence the culture in which we live. We are to be salt and light to the world around us as we penetrate the political, social and educational arenas with God's Spirit and Word.

Value Prophetic Ministries. We believe that prophecy and the ministry of the prophet are to be fully operational in the Church today. If the Church is going to be filled with vision and under the full direction of Jesus, the prophetic voice must be heard. We do not accept that this and other ministries were to be confined to an "apostolic age," but that they are to be fully activated until the physical return of Christ.

Value the Local Church. We believe that the local church is the aspect of the Church that God is focusing on building in these days. Although we all recognize and understand that the larger Body of Christ encompasses all believers, all the plans and purposes of God are going to be demonstrated and fulfilled on the local scene. Every believer must find himself or herself in right relationship to God and to a specific local church to find a place of ministry and fruitfulness. It is essential that rather than criticizing the Church, we do everything we can to make the Church of Jesus Christ glorious. The Church is God's instrument to extend His purposes on earth today.

Value Eldership Government. We believe that God has a plan and pattern for government in the local church. It is the same form of government God has used in every institution He has established. We refer to this as team ministry or an "eldership" form of government headed by a senior pastor or chief elder. This form of government involves equality and headship modeled in the Godhead, established in the natural family, set up by God in Israel, used in the synagogue and ordained for the Church in the New Testament (see Acts 14:23; Titus 1:5; Heb. 13:17). The elders are to the local church what parents are to a family. They are the spiritual parents of the local assembly and are responsible before God to establish and equip the members of the church to be able to function in their God-ordained callings.

Value the Fivefold Ministry. We believe that the ministries listed in Ephesians 4:11 are to be fully functioning right up until the return of Christ. This includes apostles and prophets, not just pastors, teachers and evangelists. All these ministries are needed if the Body of Christ is going to be properly equipped and the Church is going to be properly built up.

Value the Gifts of the Spirit. We believe that the gifts of the Spirit enumerated in 1 Corinthians 12:7-11 are not only for today, but also should be desired, sought after and evidenced in every church. If there was ever a time these gifts were needed, it is today. We do not believe that these gifts were intended only for the embryonic Church of the first hundred years. They are to be a part of the Church right up until the return of Christ for His perfected bride.

Value Unity and Diversity. We believe that every local church should be inclusive and actively seek to include all peoples of all races, ethnic origins and socioeconomic standings. The Church of Jesus Christ is a multiethnic group that has within it the seeds for demolishing the scourge of racial prejudice. God's purpose is to make all people into one for His glory.

Revival, with all its intensity and excitement, should enhance our values, not diminish them or remove them. Values and beliefs are the foundation, the unchangeable, the guarantee for a healthy future. A church or movement must keep the core values to assure survival and success from generation to generation. These are so fundamental that, if a church is to meet the challenge of a changing world, it must be prepared to change everything about itself *except* these beliefs and values as it moves through different revival rivers.

Remember the Olympic motto of 1985, "Faster, higher, stronger." This expresses perfectly the values of striving to attain God's best for our churches. As we move faster (certainly one characteristic of a revival atmosphere), we must move with well-defined values, committed to them and with a strategy to keep them healthy.

The following diagram records eight steps that state my own personal journey in coping with revival rivers as a pastor who has stepped into and drunk from each of the previous rivers we have spoken about.

EIGHT STAGES TO REVIVAL RIVERS

Renewal. The receiving of new Holy Spirit activity into a hungry soul and allowing the Holy Spirit to bring inner refreshing and remodeling of the soul as it seeks after God. Renewal is the receiving of new life and new fire into the soul of a person, a church or a city.

Receiving. The attitude needed for leaders and people to receive from other streams of churches or movements. This is an attitude that rejects exclusiveness, knowing it is the strategy of

EIGHT STAGES TO
REVIVAL RIVERS

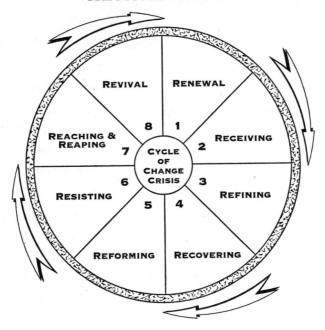

the devil to keep movements apart, thus never allowing for cross-pollination. Receiving from others, even those who are so different, is the purpose of God for His Church. The attitude that resists everything new and thinks that "we have it all" is a sure way for a church or movement to become ingrown and ulti-mately suffer spiritually.

Refining. The process of clarifying past and present truths, principles and biblical vision. When revival rivers are embraced and implemented into your own river, you must understand that revival truths or revival atmosphere might not correct a church's weaknesses. In fact, revival could expose the church's weakness and, if not dealt with wisely, bring harm to the church. Revival intensifies what is already present, so the refining process is of utmost importance.

Recovering. The ability to build upon previously laid foundations; keeping the old landmarks in truths is the guarantee of spiritual longevity.

Reforming. The process of matching new wine with new wineskins. Revival new wine usually necessitates critical time in the life of a church or ministry that embraces revival rivers. Change structure slowly for this is the bone of the church. Many churches are experiencing a restructure crisis, mobilization of lay ministry, cells, decentralization of ministry. All of these must be done with biblical priorities.

Resisting. The spiritual warfare part of revival. Every revival has this but it may be called by different names. Today's revival emphasis is on prayer intercession, spiritual mapping, identificational repentance and attacking strongholds in our cities. To implement this, a strong, healthy, local church prayer base must be established with biblical knowledge on dealing with the unseen world.

Reaching and Reaping. This is the purpose of revival, a breaking into the world of the unsaved, reaching our neighborhoods street by street until we reach whole cities for Christ. This reaching vision must be balanced with a securing of our personal, family and church borders. Revival fires may burn hot in the church to reach the city, but the same fires may burn out the workers if we do not wisely secure our borders as we reach. Evangelism fire must be balanced with a pastoral heart for the individual, family and every sheep in the flock.

Revival. This is not a word describing a special series of meetings or a spiritual experience by one or many. It is a word to describe the ongoing state of a healthy church, a church with a wide river, a river that takes in from other rivers but maintains its own river distinctives. When biblical distinctives are maintained, a church may live with a powerful, fresh, flowing river of God.

Then he brought me back to the door of the temple; and there was water, flowing from under the threshold of the temple toward the east, for the front of the temple faced east; the water was flowing from under the right side of the temple, south of the altar (Ezek. 47:1).

He brought me out by way of the north gate, and led me around on the outside to the outer gateway that faces east; and there was water, running out on the right side. And when the man went out to the east with the line in his hand, he measured one thousand cubits, and he brought me through the waters; the water came up to my ankles. Again he measured one thousand and brought me through the waters; the water came up to my knees. Again he measured one thousand and brought me through; the water came up to my waist. Again he measured one thousand, and it was a river that I could not cross; for the water was too deep, water in which one must swim, a river that could not be crossed (Ezek. 47:2-5).

He said to me, "Son of man, have you seen this?" Then he brought me and returned me to the bank of the river. When I returned, there, along the bank of the river, were very many trees on one side and the other. Then he said to me: "This water flows toward the eastern region, goes down into the valley, and enters the sea. When it reaches the sea, its waters are healed. And it shall be that every living thing that moves, wherever the rivers go, will live. There will be a very great multitude of fish, because these waters go there; for they will be healed, and everything will live wherever the river goes. It shall be that fishermen will stand by it from En Gedi to En Eglaim; they will be places for spreading their nets. Their fish will be of the same kinds as the fish of the Great Sea, exceedingly many. But its swamps and marshes will not be healed; they will be given over to salt. Along the bank of the river, on this side and that, will grow all kinds of trees used for food; their leaves will not wither, and their fruit will not fail. They will bear fruit every month, because their water flows from the sanctuary. Their fruit will be for food, and their leaves for medicine" (Ezek. 47:6-12).

And he showed me a pure river of water of life, clear as crystal, proceeding from the throne of God and of the Lamb. In the middle of its street, and on either side of the river, was the tree of life, which bore twelve fruits, each tree yielding its fruit every month. The leaves of the tree were for the healing of the nations. And there shall be no more curse, but the throne of God and of the Lamb shall be in it, and His servants shall serve Him (Rev. 22:1-3).

The rivers of revival are moving. Let us not bypass, ignore or react to them. Instead let us approach the rivers with wisdom, vision and values—a generation is at stake.

Reveal Your Glory
By Mark Strauss

Fill me with Your holy pow'r.
Touch me with Your Holy Spirit now.
Use me; Lord, I'm praying for the hour
When You reveal Your glory to me, Lord.

Lord, I ask for a mighty rushing wind;
Lord, I seek for renewal deep within;
Lord, I knock 'til You open heaven's door
And reveal Your glory to me, Lord.

Take me to Your hiding place.
Hold me; let me feel Your warm embrace.
I know I will see You face to face
When You reveal Your glory to me, Lord.[6]

PERSONAL APPLICATION

1. Revival rivers can bring both good and bad. But we must be careful not to throw the baby out with the bath water. Have you bypassed, ignored or reacted to the river rather than reaching in and removing some stones of truth?
2. Reread the list of vision values. What are some of the value commitments you need to make?
3. Which of the eight stages to revival rivers (renewal, receiving, refining, recovering, reforming, resisting, reaching and reaping, and revival) do you need to adopt as you cross the waters?

Notes
1. Winkie Pratney, *Revival Principles and Personalities* (Lafayette, LA: Hunting House Publishers, 1944), p. 11.
2. Hank Hanegraaf, *Counterfeit Revival* (Dallas: Word Publishing, 1997), p. 1.
3. Steve Hill, *The Pursuit of Revival* (Lake Mary, FL.: Creation House, 1997), pp. 2, 3.
4. John Arnott, Malcolm McDow and Alvin Reid, *Revival* (Nashville: Broadman Holman Publishers, 1996), pp. 148, 149.

5. C. Peter Wagner and Pablo Deiros, *The Rising Revival* (Ventura, CA: Renew Books), p. 13.

6. Mark Strauss, "Reveal Your Glory," City Bible Music, 1997. Used with permission.

CHAPTER 5

DISCOVERING
RIVER STONES
IN EVERY RIVER

Take for yourselves twelve stones from here,
out of the midst of the Jordan.

JOSHUA 4:3

Joshua moved to the edge of the river and prepared the people for the long-awaited crossing. The crossing of the river for the people of Israel was the doorway into their God-given vision to take the land and occupy it. They had wandered in the wilderness 40 long years; a whole generation had lived and died in the wilderness, and a whole generation was born in the wilderness. The generation born in the wilderness had more faith and vision for the new land than did the others. They had only known wilderness, dryness, murmuring and talk about the prophetic words from the past. Now it was their day, the day to cross over and begin to possess their destiny. The river crossing was the only other experience left to endure before they would finally set feet on their new inheritance.

RIVER STONES: TRUTHS DISCOVERED AND DEFINED

The Israelites had no idea of what was awaiting them in the land: walled cities, giants, testings, trials, battle after battle, casualties, death, loss of friends and family. The crossing of the river would introduce them to a new way of living and warring, a new culture. The river crossing would involve a strategy whereby the priests would find and remove 12 stones from the river and then carry them to the other side. This was not very significant at the moment of the crossing. It was just more time wasted, more work to do—find stones, lift stones, carry stones, build stones into an altar. I'm sure they were anxious to get on with the crossing of the river. What's so important about carrying stones at a time like this?

Every authentic revival river has hidden within it stones to be carried out of that river. Revival stones are truths discovered and defined as we journey through revival rivers. These stones must be kept relevant and alive in every generation as the truths discovered from the revival rivers. Joshua was to be careful not only to discover new stones, but to also keep the previous truths alive. Joshua 1:7,8 records his instructions concerning the written law and Moses' previous words of instruction:

> Only be strong and very courageous, that you may observe to do according to all the law which Moses My servant commanded you; do not turn from it to the right hand or to the left, that you may prosper wherever you go. This Book of the Law shall not depart from your

mouth, but you shall meditate in it day and night, that you may observe to do according to all that is written in it. For then you will make your way prosperous, and then you will have good success.

Joshua was to be careful to do all that was already written and to also discover 12 new stones from the river he was to cross. We could liken the law, or words of Moses, to our committed vision values (see chapter 4) that should be word-based, timeless principles that we build on during all seasons. Leaders and churches today must know these biblically based values and meditate upon them because our success and longevity is connected to these truths.

At the same time, we must not limit our future to what was discovered in the past. Our responsibility is to move forward and, at times, cross over revival rivers discovering the stones of truth we should carry out from these rivers.

Joshua 4:3 states our personal responsibility: "Take for yourselves twelve stones." Revival-truth stones are costly stones personally carried and protected by those who cross through the river. They are revival-discovered truths that are spiritually and personally embraced by the leader and the people. These revival-river truths become spiritual tools, convictions, birthed into and spiritually owned by the leaders and the people of revival.

"Take for yourselves twelve stones from here, out of the midst of the Jordan, from the place where the priests' feet stood firm" (Josh. 4:3). The priests' feet stood firm; the feet stood on dry ground, on a firm and stable place. Even though we pass through revival rivers, we must keep our feet on the dry ground of truth (see Josh. 3:17). This dry ground is the ground of principles, doctrine and objective truth, truths that become foundations, our belief systems. We stand on dry ground, resisting all opposition to past and present truth.

During revival seasons, the subjective is usually heightened because the Holy Spirit is moving upon people's lives in a fresh and new way. As people encounter revival rivers, they are refreshed, renewed in mind and spirit, easily brought to repentance and genuinely changed. The dry ground of objective truth balances the river of subjective experiences. The following diagram illustrates our constant need for balancing the subjective and the objective.

SUBJECTIVE	**OBJECTIVE**
INCREASE OF SUBJECTIVE EXPERIENCES	**INCREASE OF OBJECTIVE TRUTH**
CHARISMATIC PENTECOSTAL INCREASE 	**DECREASE OF SCHOLARSHIP**
DECREASE OF SPIRITUAL, SUBJECTIVE EXPERIENCES	**EVANGELICAL MAINLINE DENOMINATIONS INCREASE SCHOLARSHIP**

As we pass through these waters of various revival rivers, our responsibility is to find stones, truths that will outlast the experience, emotion and intensity of the moment. Every revival must have a Bible base, a truth or truths, that carry the revival.

In the past, authentic revivals were marked by newly found truths: justification by faith, holiness, Holy Spirit baptism or infilling of the Holy Spirit, sanctification, gifts of the Spirit, missionary fervor, new realms of prayer and fasting.

As we pass through the river, we must discover and define the river stones, not just the depth of the water, the power of the current or the beauty of the flow. We must discover the foundational truths that validate the river as being authentic. These are the stones we must discover and then carry out for the next generation to remember and use as they build for the future. We as spiritual leaders must "take up a stone on our shoulder" and bear these truths as personal burdens if necessary. These truths may be controversial, causing others to attack the truth and the person carrying the truth.

MOTIVATED BY LOVE FOR THE GENERATION "NEXT"

Our motivation must be the next generation. Revival stones are directional stones for the next generation. Joshua 4:6 says, "That this may be a sign among you when your children ask in time to come, saying, 'What do these stones mean to you?'" River truths are only fresh to the generation that first discovers and carries them on their shoulders. These same truths are not automatically accepted, respected and kept alive by the next generation. River truths must be explained, imparted and carefully placed into the next generation. Leonard Sweet, in his book *Eleven Genetic Gateways to Spiritual Awakening*, addresses this generational problem of spiritual decline in his denomination, the Methodists:

> We suffered 48 percent loss in our market share in the past half century. If the chief purpose of a community

of faith is to pass on its tradition to its children, we are facing a reproduction crisis of the highest order. The old prophecy, the church always stands one generation away from extinction has almost been self-fulfilled.[1]

Leadership must carry river truths across every new era and every new river, laying them down in their new resting place, a new generation:

> And the children of Israel did so, just as Joshua commanded, and took up twelve stones from the midst of the Jordan, as the LORD had spoken to Joshua, according to the number of the tribes of the children of Israel, and carried them over with them to the place where they lodged, and laid them down there (Josh. 4:8).

River stones discovered in the river must be symbolically kept in the river. The river of God's presence, anointing and life must be the sustaining power of all river truths. If these truths were discovered in the presence and power of God, they must be kept by the presence and power of God. If river truths are separated from the river's power, they have the potential of becoming dead orthodoxy, dead letters without life-giving power. They may be documented and well-articulated but without the original power and life they will not capture a new generation. The life of the teaching is in the life of the teacher.

There is a story of a spring of water that possessed extraordinary medicinal properties. Those who drank of its healing streams were miraculously cured of their diseases and infirmities. The news of this incredible find spread like wildfire, so multitudes came from far and wide to experience this phenomenal happening. Many erected homes beside the healing spring. Before long, hotels and businesses were also erected around the healing spring. The town grew into a city, and the city became a great buzz of activity.

Finally, there came a day when visitors would come to the city and ask, "Where in this great city is the pure spring of water that flows with healing power?"

With deep humiliation the residents were forced to reply, "We are so sorry, but somehow in the midst of our progress and advancement, we lost the spring. Now, we cannot find it!" They lost the purpose of their existence.

The 12 stones taken from the river are spiritually quickened biblical truths—truths that may have lain dormant but now, by the power of the Holy Spirit, come alive during revival times. Allow me to name the 12 stones that I have taken from these present revival rivers, as have countless other river people. These are not the only stones to discover afresh from revival rivers, but they represent the testimony of many people.

TWELVE STONES THAT WE HAVE TAKEN FROM THE RIVER

1. THE STONE OF HUMILITY AND SIMPLICITY

The Bible places a high value on humility and childlikeness. God saves (see Ps. 18:27), sustains (see Ps. 147:6), and gives grace to the humble (see Prov. 3:34). Humbled before God, we are able to experience all the blessings He has for us. This stone is evident in every revival stream I have touched—stronger in some than others, but still present. Humility and simplicity, accessible to all who would see them as valuable, are God's gateway to receiving from any of His true servants: male or female, any race or color, small church ministry or large church ministry, clergyman or layman. All are conduits of God's Holy Spirit. When the disciples asked Jesus who was the greatest in the kingdom of heaven (see Matt.

18:1-4), Jesus simply called to a little child and instructed the disciples to become like the child. Whoever humbles himself or herself like a child will be the greatest.

On several occasions at various revival hot spots, I have received from people who weren't the speakers or really any part of the leadership team visible on the platform. They were merely kind, gentle people filled with faith and desiring to be used of God as a channel of blessing. I must admit that my first thoughts were usually, *Who is this person and what can he/she do? This person is not even a full-time minister. How could this person understand my needs as a clergyman? What does this person have to give? I would rather have the keynote speaker pray for me. After all, does he/she realize who I am?* This thinking is what the Bible calls pride, the opposite of humility, and is the attitude that hinders God from using others to bless (see Eph. 4:2; Phil. 2:5-8).

Leaders from all around the world have testified to the stone of humility and simplicity as a new truth, a new experience, for them. It breaks something down inside leaders. Their hearts are changed and this revival stone is used to provide a gateway to their own congregations (see Rom. 12:3-16).

2. THE STONE OF IMPARTATION

Impartation has taken on a new meaning for thousands of people in the last few years. Never have so many people been prayed for by so many people expecting to receive something. Impartation is a biblical word with biblical illustration throughout Scripture. Deuteronomy 34:9 says, "Now Joshua the son of Nun was full of the spirit of wisdom, for Moses had laid his hands on him." The impartation was real. It was tangible. Something happened to Joshua when Moses laid his hands on him.

In 2 Kings 2:9 we read, "And so it was, when they had crossed over, that Elijah said to Elisha, 'Ask! What may I do for you, before I am taken away from you?' Elisha said, 'Please let a double portion of your spirit be upon me.'" Again we see the principle of impartation. Elisha expected to receive, and Elijah had faith to impart from his life.

Impartation means to deposit, giving of something to another, to place into (see Gal. 1:16; 2:6). Romans 1:11 reads, "For I long to see you, that I may impart to you some spiritual gift, so that you may be established." The revival rivers flowing today have used this truth to minister to multiplied thousands. It is a revival stone we should pick up, put on our shoulders and carry out of the river. There seems to be a new level of faith in people to receive from others, a new expectation.

3. THE STONE OF INTERCESSORY PRAYER

Everywhere you go, everywhere you look, you find books, tapes, seminars, conferences, magazines, churches with prayer pastors, prayer mountains, all-night prayer watches and prayer movements. Prayer has moved to a new level. Prayer intercession has been a part of all past revivals and certainly is a part of the new revivals throughout the world.

The World Prayer Center in Colorado Springs under the ministry of Dr. C. Peter Wagner has just opened with state-of-the-art computers and communications to link thousands of intercessors around the world. This ministry will help intercessory prayer become a laser beam in praying with knowledge and strategy. A new magazine called *Pray: Encouraging a Passion for Prayer* has found great receptivity because of today's worldwide prayer movement. In the September/October 1998 issue, one article is entitled "100,000 Intercessors Wanted." This was just for one nation—France!

The revival stone of intercessory prayer will revolutionize your life, ministry and church. When I first came in contact with the different revival rivers, I was most overwhelmed with the spirit of intercessory prayer. The Holy Spirit would move thousands of people into a level of prayer intercession not previously known, at least by me or our church. As God dealt with me, and ultimately our whole congregation, we spent months teaching and practicing intercessory prayer.

We now have opening service prayer intercession in which the whole church enters into a prayer intercession for the first 20 minutes of the service and then moves into worship and the Word. We have a prayer center, a prayer pastor, 400 trained and assigned prayer intercessors. We picked up this stone, put it on our shoulders and are carrying it out of the river.

Our mission statement concerning this newly discovered river stone of intercessory prayer is:

- Inspire every believer's heart toward prayer intercession through the Word of God, stories, principles and prayer models.
- Impart seeds of God's Word concerning prayer intercession that will produce a great harvest of prayer.
- Impact each and every member of our congregation with a vision to change cities, nations and history through prayer intercession.
- Influence every believer toward prayer intercession that stands in the gap and builds hedges for our families, churches, cities and nations.
- Increase the faith of every believer to understand and utilize prayer as a powerful weapon to bring down spiritual strongholds and thus reap an awesome harvest of souls.

(See Exod. 32:11-14; 1 Kings 18:41-46; Esther 5:1-3; Ezek. 22:30; Luke 2:37.)

4. THE STONE OF RECONCILING THE GENERATIONS

Each generation must receive its own distinct spiritual encounter with God. As generations come and go, they each bear certain dominant distinctions that are the result of cultural trends and spiritual powers. The Church is responsible for past, present and emerging generations. We now face the rising of another generation which, for various reasons, some call Generation X. Generation X is so titled because it is considered the invisible generation without notable, easily defined, dominant characteristics.

Born between 1965 and 1980, these are the post baby boomers. This generation has been called the "re-generation," which lacks identity and thus creates one by reviving or repeating the past. Descriptions for this generation are numerous: slackers, grunge kids, tweeners, late-bloomers, post-boomers, boom-erang generation, disillusioned generation, and so on. The point is obvious: We have a generation that desperately needs an encounter with an authentic Christ, an authentic Church, and authentic spiritual mentors and leaders.

Revival fires have warmed the hearts of thousands to reach this generation and reconcile past and present genera-tions. One insightful Generation Xer paints a vivid picture of our challenge and the true heart attitude of millions in this age group: "Searching desperately for godly mentors to teach us, yet not knowing where to look, we are feeling like runners stranded at the starting gate without a baton. Some may characterize us as lazy slackers, but the truth is that ours is a traumatized generation, lacking direction and identity—missing a sense of continuity with our heritage."[2] There is a stone in these present revival rivers, a stone of burden, intercessory prayer and Holy Spirit strategy to reach the next generation.

5. THE STONE OF RESTORING MEN TO
TAKE RESPONSIBILITY

The revival among the men of our nation is both encouraging and challenging. The Promise Keepers organization has taken the lead in gathering men by the millions nationwide to become godly men who embrace responsibility. The present moving of the Holy Spirit will best be sustained if we pick up this stone and carry it out of the river—the stone of equipping and releasing men into their God-called position.

No other group of individuals has more power to shape or change the flow of history and spiritual life in our world today. If men do not receive biblical training on how to take their biblical place and fulfill biblical responsibility, we will miss what God is seeking to do in our day. John Wesley's famous proclamation was, "Give me one hundred men who love God and hate sin, and we will shake the gates of Hell."[3]

Women have been marching along for 20 to 30 years with men standing by and watching the parade. God has certainly given men a wake-up call, and it is of great importance that spiritual leaders pick up the stone of men's ministries, men's groups, men's training, men's roles in marriage and relationships, and carry this stone out of the river. Promise Keepers and other men's organizations may be strong for several years or several decades, but we must understand that the Church is here to stay. The men's revival must take place in our churches, not just in a stadium.

I have called the men in our church to pursue godly priorities. The following acronym of the word "priority" serves as a guide and reminder to our men that we are God-pursuers (see Ps. 63:1-5).

Pursuing Our God: The command of Jesus was to seek first the kingdom of God. The psalmist says, pant after God, thirst for God (see Ps. 42), and seek God earnestly (see Ps. 63). To pursue God is to practice the discipline of earnest prayer and to keep a single focus.

Rebuilding Altars: To build an altar is to express a special kind of dedication toward God. The altars we build are reflections of our spiritual state and attitude.

Investing Our Lives: Our joys, successes and fulfillment in life are determined by the degree to which we discover God's purpose for our lives, invest ourselves in that purpose, and then use our talents, possessions, time and energy to fulfill that purpose.

Overcoming Consistently: The power to overcome the habits of the flesh is found in understanding the right biblical principles and applying those principles by the power of the Holy Spirit. Victory is possible. It is promised in Scripture to those who discover and apply truth (see Rom. 6:14).

Removing Obstacles: Long-standing obstacles must be removed in order for spiritual growth and progress to take place. Determine what they are, name them and remove them. Common obstacles revealed in the Scripture are doubt, discouragement, rebellion, covetousness, an unruly tongue and focusing on the pleasures of this life.

Invading Enemy Territory: Now is the time to go in and win back territory the enemy has taken in your life. Israel was given an inheritance in Canaan, but Joshua had to lead the people in and fight for it. Invading enemy territory takes vision, faith and warfare.

Thinking Triumphantly: Train your mind to think godly thoughts based on the Word of God and inspired by the Spirit of God. Bad habits are the product of bad thoughts.

Yielding Successfully: Yield all ownership and rights to God, recognizing Him as Lord and yourself as His servant.

6. THE STONE OF HEALING AND MIRACLES

Most authentic revivals have borne witness to notable healings and miracles. The healing ministry has always been one with significant controversy, and yet it has been part of the Christian Church for centuries. Participants in revivals around the world maintain the belief that physical, mental and emotional illnesses can be cured by the supernatural intervention of God through the prayer of faith. This stone must be grasped and held on to if we are to see healings and miracles move from the conferences and convention centers into our local churches.

The river of revival has come to reveal the stones in the rivers—stones to build with, not to walk over, forget and neglect. The healing stone is desperately needed in every local church across this and every other nation. The power of the Lord to heal today is the same as it was in the day Christ walked upon the face of the earth (see Isa. 53:5; Heb. 13:8). The ministry of Christ as stated in Luke 4:16-19 is the same ministry the Church has today:

- To heal the brokenhearted;
- To deliver the captives;
- To heal the blind;
- To set free the blind;
- To set free the bruised;
- To comfort the mourning;
- To give beauty for ashes;
- To give the garment of praise for heaviness.

The river of revival has refreshed our spirits and opened our eyes to this power stone lying at our feet. A stone of healing must be picked up by every leader and every prayer (see Matt. 4:23-25; 8:7; 9:35; Luke 6:17-19). Many have crossed the rivers of revival before us bearing the healing stone with awesome results: A. B.

Simpson, Alexander Dowie, Charles Parham, Aimee Semple MacPherson, Dr. Charles Price, F. F. Bosworth, Andrew Murray, Oral Roberts, and many, many more.

Every local congregation needs a healing theology that is known and believed by the entire congregation. The following is one that I have used for years. It is simple and straight to the point of receiving your healing:

- Believe that healing is biblical, for today and for you (see Ps. 103:2; Isa. 53:1-3; Matt. 8:17; 1 Pet. 2:24).
- Believe that Christ's ministry of healing is now through His people (see Matt. 9:29; Mark 6:1-6; Jas. 1:6).
- Ask for the anointing of oil and prayer by the elders (see Jas. 5:14; Matt. 6:13; Luke 13:11-13; Acts 28:8).
- Believe in faith that nothing is too hard for the Lord (see Jer. 32:17; Matt. 8:2-4; 9:22,29; 17:20; Mark 9:23; 10:27; 16:17).

Now, you must pray for the sick—continually, consistently, when it doesn't work, and when people shove it off as, *Oh well, I guess it's not for today.* Peter Wagner says in his book *How to Have a Healing Ministry in Any Church*, "If people believe that God does not heal today, they will not be able to see divine healing, no matter what quantity of documentation or proof is provided."[4] Let us prayerfully and carefully carry this great stone from the revival rivers of yesterday and today.

7. THE STONE OF HOLINESS

Most revivals discover this truth as foundational to Holy Spirit activity. (See Heb. 12:14; 1 Pet. 1:15,16.) Revivals of the past have preached and written volumes on holiness. It is a new fresh Holy Spirit thought for a new generation. Some of the holiness teachings of the past have resulted in a dead-letter holiness, a legalism resisted by another generation emerging. Legalism that robs Christians of their true freedom in Christ is not the holiness of Scripture.

Legalism is an attitude. Although it involves code, motive and power, it is basically an attitude. Legalism may be defined as a fleshly attitude that conforms to a code for the purpose of exalting self. Legalism as an attitude is founded in pride and becomes obsessive with conforming to artificial standards for the purpose of exalting self. Legalism results in illegitimate control, requiring unanimity, not unity. Legalism is the manipulation of rules for the purpose of illegitimate control.

Legalism as an attitude is found in pride and

becomes obsessive with conforming to artificial

standards for the purpose of exalting self.

Legalism results in illegitimate control, requiring

unanimity, not unity.

In most revival meetings I have attended, I have heard several testimonies about leaders releasing control. The word "control" is actually mentioned quite often in revival literature, tapes and conferences. I believe control is linked to a legalistic spirit, a spirit that is deadened by religiosity and formalistic-driven ministry. When true Holy Spirit renewal invades a person's soul, this deadness is driven out and a new spirit of grace, mercy and love takes residence with a new motivation for serving Christ and His people.

When grace fills a human soul, holiness becomes a vision, an automatic new drive, and a desire to be free from anything that would hinder a first-love relationship with Jesus. Throughout the New Testament the predominant thought is the grace of God in which Christ releases us, governs us and gives a new hope and a new vision for our lives. As we see in Titus 2:11-14, the grace of God and the holiness of God are brought together in the believer's experience:

> For the grace of God that brings salvation has appeared to all men, teaching us that, denying ungodliness and worldly lusts, we should live soberly, righteously, and godly in the present age, looking for the blessed hope and glorious appearing of our great God and Savior Jesus Christ, who gave Himself for us, that He might redeem us from every lawless deed and purify for Himself His own special people, zealous for good works.

Grace has appeared, bringing salvation and motivating the believer toward a new discipline—holiness. Grace motivates us to deny ungodliness, deny worldly desires and live sensibly and righteously. The Holy Spirit has once again enlightened our eyes to see this stone in the river so that we might bend over, pick it up and carry it over to the other side.

8. THE STONE OF RACIAL RECONCILIATION

John Dawson says in his book *Healing America's Wounds*, "America's cities are now the greatest gatherings of ethnic and cultural diversity the world has ever seen. We have inherited the wounds of the world, the clash of ancient rivalries, and we have our own unfinished business, particularly with Native Americans and Afro-Americans."[5] The unfinished business that Dawson speaks about is racial reconciliation, a forgiving and reconciling of the injustices which races have incurred upon each other, whether from days past or present.

Second Corinthians 5:18-20 reads: "Now all things are of God, who has reconciled us to Himself through Jesus Christ, and has given us the ministry of reconciliation, that is, that God was in Christ reconciling the world to Himself, not imputing their trespasses to them, and has committed to us the word of reconciliation. Now then, we are ambassadors for Christ, as though God were pleading through us: we implore you on Christ's behalf, be reconciled to God."

This passage literally means that we have been called to be servants of reconciliation. Servants are those who yield their rights, submit to those over them and sacrificially give themselves to the cause. God has and is speaking forcefully and forthrightly concerning racial reconciliation—it is a stone of truth you will find in present revival rivers.

Racial reconciliation is now being emphasized by several groups. It is a God-word for this present time. As the world sits in racial hostility, the Church is being called to racial reconciliation. For some, this has been a hard stone to see in the river. Many think, *Not me, I've done nothing to these people. Should I need to ask forgiveness even though I wasn't present when they were enslaved, brutalized or forced to give up their land? Why should I feel guilty?*

Of all peoples, Christians should be concerned about racial strife, conflict and roots of bitterness. This issue is surely one of the most fundamental social problems of our time. In *Breaking Strongholds*, authors Raleigh Washington and Glen Kehrem quote Diane Sawyer's interview with Billy Graham on "Prime Time Live": "If you could wave your hand and make one problem in this world go away, what would that be?" Without pausing for breath Dr. Graham quickly replied, "Racial division and strife."[6]

The racial reconciliation stone must be picked up by every leader and every congregation. It is time to pick up our crosses, step out of our comfort zones and build relationships across cultural barriers, beginning with at least one person, one family, one church.

When I finally understood and accepted this stone as a present truth, a Holy Spirit-inspired thought for the Church today, I moved toward making racial reconciliation a real livable truth for myself and our congregation. I needed to reconcile within my own heart first, "Yes, I am American. And even though I wasn't here 200 years ago, my ancestors committed horrible sins against the Chinese, Native American and African-American people. This fact is part of my past, my heritage; therefore, it is my responsibility to ask for forgiveness and to work toward removing the hatred, the bitterness and the long taproot of injustice."

I began with one African-American pastor, then two, then three, building relationships on a monthly basis through lunches, prayer meetings, city communion services, helping churches made up of other races with finances, staffing, legal help—anything I could do to strengthen the relationship between the races. It has been a learning experience. I, like many other white pastors, was totally ignorant of how to love the African-American and I truly did not understand their frame of reference. I was frustrated and critical, thinking, *Surely it can't be that bad. Why don't they just give it up? It happened 100 years ago!* The journey is still going on, yet I am different. I know how far we still must go, but at least we have begun.

Racial reconciliation is one of the most important stones you will find in the river. Don't kick it, ignore it or just touch it.

Pick it up, own it and carry it. Educate yourself. Begin by reading books and listening to tapes on the subject, or better yet, start where you are with one other person of a different race. I highly recommend reading *Breaking Strongholds* by Washington and Kehrem and *Healing America's Wounds* by John Dawson.

9. THE STONE OF STRATEGIC-LEVEL SPIRITUAL WARFARE

Spiritual warfare is not a new term to most Bible-believing Christians. True born-again believers understand that there is a real devil, who has real demonic forces at his command and wicked spirits in high places that wage war against people. Most Christians understand this kind of spiritual attack on a personal level, but many turn a deaf ear in unbelief when confronted with the concept that spiritual powers in high places control cities, regions and nations.

Peter Wagner presents three levels of spiritual warfare in his book, *Warfare Prayer:*

First is ground-level spiritual warfare. This is the ministry of casting out demons as stated in Matthew 10:1: "And when He had called His twelve disciples to Him, He gave them power over unclean spirits, to cast them out, and to heal all kinds of sickness and all kinds of disease." Groups and individuals in deliverance ministries by and large are engaged in ground-level spiritual warfare.

The second level is occult-level spiritual warfare. It seems evident that we see demonic powers at work through shamans, New Age channelers, occult practitioners, witches and warlocks, Satanist priests, fortune-tellers and the like. Word that the number of registered witches in Germany exceeds the number of registered Christian clergy is startling. Hard data is elusive, but in all probability the most rapidly growing religious movement in America is New Age.

The third level of spiritual warfare is strategic-level spiritual warfare. Here we contend with an even more ominous concentration of demonic forces and powers—territorial spirits. This level of spiritual warfare has taken on new interest and new focus. City evangelism and strategic-level spiritual warfare becomes a top priority when taking our cities for Christ. The terminology that has surfaced over the last several years involves terms like spiritual mapping, breaking strongholds, city-reaching warfare, and strategic-level warfare, all of which have varying meanings to different people.[7]

Our journey into reaching our city has led us into prayer intercession, spiritual warfare and spiritual strategies. When I first learned about spiritual mapping, I was, like many other believers, a little hesitant to put much stock in it. How can anyone use normal means to understand spiritual problems, spiritual strongholds, principalities and powers? However, as we have researched and implemented strategic-prayer intercession, we have discovered that gaining a spiritual understanding of our city, region and state has become very important.

Harold Caballeros, in his book *The Transforming Power of Revival*, tells the story of how spiritual mapping led him to understand the power over Guatemala, the god worshiped by the first inhabitants. Guatemala had been offered and dedicated to a principality called Quetzalcoatl, the feathered snake. To begin spiritual warfare, one had to name the principality over the land that exercises its power through concepts, ideas or ideologies (see 2 Cor. 10:3-5). Caballeros says that spiritual mapping is equivalent to intelligence gathering or espionage in war.[8]

Spiritual mapping is for the intercessors what an X ray is for a doctor; it is a means for diagnosing the spiritual reality that affects our communities. This is precisely why we as leaders in our nation must pick up this spiritual stone: the stone of strategic-level warfare through strategic intercession. This is not an end in itself; it is a means to our end—evangelism, the winning of souls to Christ.

If you knew that spiritual mapping, along with prayer intercession, with balanced biblical warfare would result in the tearing down of spiritual strongholds in your city and releasing souls from hell's grip, would you not use this weapon? I think you would because you desire to see souls come to Christ in every region. Obviously other ingredients are also needed to shake a city for Christ besides spiritual warfare on this level, but spiritual mapping is an effective weapon available to the twenty-first-century Church.

We Americans are deceived if we think spiritual mapping is needed more in the dark countries of our world—countries with witches, warlocks, curses, demons, pagan belief systems, idol worship, et cetera—than in our own. Our nation is as dark, if not darker, than most. Spiritual powers are at work capturing the souls of people, and where is the Church? The Church, for the most part, is content to stay within its four walls singing hymns to one another, running church programs and speaking great messages against the darkness all around it.

Don't you believe the time has come to attack, invade and push back the dark powers that are destroying our unborn babies, our youth and our homes? The spirit of homosexuality has grown to the extent that it now influences the media, politics, education and philosophy. We must strategically push back the invisible powers, know what they are, where they are, and how to defeat them. This is a stone in the river that we cannot afford to mishandle. We must hold it tight and move on.

10. THE STONE OF SECURING TOTAL FREEDOM FOR BELIEVERS AND UNBELIEVERS

I have been in the ministry for almost a quarter of a century serving as a youth pastor, associate pastor, Bible college professor, church planter, and now as the senior pastor of City Bible Church and president of Portland Bible College. My journey has allowed me to be on the ground level of new believers, new churches, new leaders and new movements.

The one very vivid picture that stands out in my mind is the picture of someone bound with huge chains and crying out for help. As I walk around surveying this person, I try different keys to the locks. "No, not this key. Let's try this one. No. How about this formula?" This is a picture of frustrated spiritual leaders desiring to set people free, but not possessing the right keys.

Somewhere along the Church's journey, a significant part of Jesus' ministry has been dropped—His deliverance ministry—the ministry that set people free, broke the invisible demonic chains off people's souls, cast out demons and broke off the spirits of infirmity. This part of Christ's ministry has been theologically assassinated and slowly but surely removed from Bible colleges and seminaries. You will not find Casting Out Demons 101 in today's training institutions. We teach young leaders how to preach, teach, administrate, counsel and research, but when do we teach them the power of deliverance and how to set the captives free? Most see deliverance as an unpopular practice of ministry that can be replaced with psychology. Deliverance is not being practiced by multiplied thousands of our American churches, and the result is that thousands of both believers and unbelievers are living in spiritual bondage.

The Scripture says, "[We] will cast out demons" (Mark 16:17). Argentine evangelist Carlos Annacondia has modeled Jesus' ministry of deliverance and taking authority over evil spiritual powers. In his new book *Listen to Me, Satan!* on exercising authority over the devil in Jesus' name, Annacondia says, "Demons are evil beings who have no material bodies, and they go around looking for a place to dwell. They speak, they reason, they see, and they hear."[9] Annacondia believes Jesus has given the believer authority to deal with these demonic forces that torment, oppress or possess people. We have a great need to learn from this Argentine brother and many others south of the border.

Another approach to bringing total freedom to those suffering from chronic spiritual disorders is the "Cleansing Stream Seminar" out of Jack Hayford's The Church On The Way. This ministry's mission statement reads: "Paul challenges us, and the Holy Spirit, speaking through Him, commands us to be people who walk in the Spirit. Unfortunately, because we see our shortcomings, the failures of the past, the sins we have committed, and the hurts and pains of our lives, the thought of fulfilling such a command overwhelms us."[10]

The Cleansing Stream Seminar deals with finding and securing your freedom in body, soul and spirit through prayers of deliverance, confession of sins, releasing bitterness and tearing down soul strongholds. The Holy Spirit is using this approach to free multiplied thousands of believers who are living in some level of spiritual bondage.

Another trumpet-sounding message of securing your personal deliverance is Neil Anderson in his two companion books *Victory over the Darkness* and *The Bondage Breaker*. In *The Bondage Breaker*, Anderson states his purpose: "I have attempted to clarify the nature of spiritual conflicts and outline how they can be resolved in Christ. Part one explains your position of freedom, protection, and authority in Christ. Part two warns of your vulnerability to very real and very personal demonic influences which are intent on robbing you of your freedom through temptation, accusations, deception, and control."[11]

Our culture is demonized, harassed and tormented with multiple addictions to drugs, alcohol, pornography and materialism. Surely we understand our spiritual condition and the absolute necessity for deliverance ministry. This river stone of truth must be picked up by local church leadership and placed into the local church congregation. Deliverance ministry should be part of the defined purpose and function of every local church. Deliverance counseling, deliverance prayer centers and deliverance meetings are growing in our nation. Let us be wise and make room for this vital ministry under the covering of the local church.

Our local church eldership has spent months researching, reading available books, locating churches that have functioning deliverance ministries, and pounding out a basic deliverance ministry theology, philosophy and function. Our basic line of thinking would be represented in this opening statement in one of our research studies given to the eldership of our church:

Demonology has been a controversial subject in the Body of Christ for quite some time. It seems that Christians tend to move to one of two extremes: either overemphasizing the existence and power of Satan and his forces, or denying or ignoring his existence and power. In some Christian gatherings, you may hear as much or more said about Satan and demons as about God and the power of the gospel. However, in other churches you would hardly ever hear a reference to the kingdom of darkness. We tend to either become demon chasers or powerless wonders. We are certainly in need of gaining a balanced perspective of the truth concerning this subject.

Our goal, however, must not only include becoming biblically informed (see John 8:32), but also being spiritually empowered (see Luke 10:19). We want the power of the truth and Spirit to permeate our experience, but we should not make the mistake of basing our doctrine on our experiences. Our five senses and natural observations should be deemed inadequate to always accurately discern and define what is true in the spiritual realm, particularly in relation to the kingdom of darkness where the modus operandi is deception. Obviously, the Word of God is the only solid rock we have as the foundation for our understanding. May we be thoroughly equipped by it unto every good work (see 2 Tim. 3:16,17).

11. THE STONE OF REAPING A RIPE HARVEST BOTH LOCALLY AND GLOBALLY

The word "harvest" implies the season of gathering in a ripened crop, a time of reaping that which is mature. The Holy Spirit is certainly speaking through many leaders around the world that now is the time of harvest, thrust in your sickle for the harvest is ripe. In Luke 10:2 Jesus pleads, "The harvest truly is great, but the laborers are few; therefore pray the Lord of the harvest to send out laborers into His harvest."

Positioning the Church for evangelism goes beyond implementing a program or hiring additional staff. Ultimately it takes a corporate change of heart. In my estimation, this is the purpose of the Holy Spirit's outpouring upon the Church: a change of heart toward the lost. The Church potentially may become a bread bakery, working hard to make bread, package bread, strategize the marketing of bread while neglecting the starving, dying people looking through the glass at the bread.

The Holy Spirit through revival is igniting the hearts of people with fire, fires of love, mercy and passion for our lost, hurting and dying world. The worldwide proclamation of the gospel awaits accomplishments by a generation that will have the obedience, courage and determination to attempt the task. A harvest passion

The Church may become a bread bakery,

working hard to make bread, package

bread, strategize the marketing of bread

while neglecting the starving, dying people

looking through the glass at the bread.

affects our preaching, teaching, worship, prayers, budgets, programs and hearts. A harvest passion will change our vision for ourselves, our children, our personal finances, our time and our life goals. This passion will drive us from our religious comfort zones into a war zone, a place where we do battle for the souls of others. Our lives, our philosophies and our values are deeply impacted and strategically changed by a harvest passion. The revival fires we see blazing around the globe all have this fire burning hot and spreading.

The Lausanne Committee's motto some years back was, "The whole Church must take the whole gospel to the whole world!" The Holy Spirit is quickening the following harvest Scriptures so that we might meditate upon them and allow Him to use them to build a fresh new passion and faith within us for the ripened harvest:

> Then Jesus went about all the cities and villages, teaching in their synagogues, preaching the gospel of the kingdom, and healing every sickness and every disease among the people. But when He saw the multitudes, He was moved with compassion for them, because they were weary and scattered, like sheep having no shepherd. Then He said to His disciples, "The harvest truly is plentiful, but the laborers are few" (Matt. 9:35-37).

> "Let both grow together until the harvest, and at the time of harvest I will say to the reapers, 'First gather together the tares and bind them in bundles to burn them, but gather the wheat into my barn'" (Matt. 13:30).

> "But when the grain ripens, immediately he puts in the sickle, because the harvest has come" (Mark 4:29).

> "Do you not say, 'There are still four months and then comes the harvest'? Behold, I say to you, lift up your eyes and look at the fields, for they are already white for harvest! And he who reaps receives wages, and gathers fruit for eternal life, that both he who sows and he who reaps may rejoice together. For in this the saying is true: 'One sows and another reaps.' I sent you to reap that for which you have not labored; others have labored, and you have entered into their labors" (John 4:35-38).

> And He said to them, "It is not for you to know times or seasons which the Father has put in His own authority.

But you shall receive power when the Holy Spirit has come upon you; and you shall be witnesses to Me in Jerusalem, and in all Judea and Samaria, and to the end of the earth" (Acts 1:7,8).

"Go therefore and make disciples of all the nations, baptizing them in the name of the Father and of the Son and of the Holy Spirit" (Matt. 28:19).

Then I looked, and I heard the voice of many angels around the throne, the living creatures, and the elders; and the number of them was ten thousand times ten thousand, and thousands of thousands (Rev. 5:11).

After these things I looked, and behold, a great multitude which no one could number, of all nations, tribes, peoples, and tongues, standing before the throne and before the Lamb, clothed with white robes, with palm branches in their hands, and crying out with a loud voice, saying, "Salvation belongs to our God who sits on the throne, and to the Lamb!" (Rev. 7:9,10).

Then I saw another angel flying in the midst of heaven, having the everlasting gospel to preach to those who dwell on the earth—to every nation, tribe, tongue, and people (Rev. 14:6).

Churches in revival will dig into the river and find this precious "reaping a ripe harvest" stone, pick it up, hold it tightly, and carry it securely, for it is foundational to the sustaining of revival in any city or nation. Every church must see the vision of ordinary people going into ordinary places to reap an extraordinary harvest. A church vision for the harvest must develop a harvest philosophy, a harvest value system that is owned by the corporate church, a harvest passion in every believer.

HARVEST PASSION

Passion is defined as hot love, fervor or intensity, hot emotion, excitement, to be stirred, awakened, energized, to be set on fire. The following are slang expressions used to describe passion: to touch a chord, go to one's heart, touch to the quick, turn one's head, sweep off one's feet. The opposite of passion is inactive, untouched, unemotional, unstirred, indifferent, neutral, sluggishness. As you read these words, which ones describe your heart for the harvest? Which ones describe your church atmosphere? God is calling His people to a holy passion.

Achieving God's best requires a wholehearted abandonment. Every person who ever accomplished anything significant had this biblical ingredient—zeal, passion, a hot heart. Passion enabled past and present heroes to overcome all obstacles in pursuit of the goal. William Carey, missionary to India, said, "Attempt great things for God. Expect great things from God."[12] The elements of contagious intensity and on-fire mission, impassioned with the task ahead are what motivated heaven's Hall of Famers to give their all, even their very lives: George Whitefield said, "Give me souls or I will die."[13] "Now let me burn out for God!" cried Henry Martyn as he stood on Indian soil for the first time.[14] David Brainerd stated in his journal, "Consumed with passion for the pagan Indians, I cared not when or how I lived or what hardships I endured so that I could gain souls for Christ. While I was asleep I dreamt of such things, and when I awakened the first thing I thought of was winning souls to Christ."[15]

Jesus said in John 4:32,34: "I have food to eat of which you do not know.... My food is to do the will of Him who sent Me, and to finish His work." This was His hidden source of spiritual nourishment, His hidden motor, His hidden well that He drew from continually.

The Church of the twenty-first century is in need of biblical passion:

- A passion that seizes harvest opportunities continually (see John 9:35).
- A passion that views the harvest attentively (see John 4:35).
- A passion that reaps the harvest aggressively (see John 4:35).
- A passion that possesses the harvest immediately (see John 4:35).
- A passion that labors in the harvest perceptively (see John 4:36).
- A passion that loves the harvest deeply (see John 4:36).

It has been estimated that we spend $600 on luxuries for every $1 we spend on missions. We have a nation that spends more on tobacco in one year than the United States and Canada combined have spent on missions since Columbus discovered America. Even if these figures are not exact, anything within reach of them is still staggering to comprehend.

A HARVEST PHILOSOPHY

The Church must adopt a harvest philosophy:

- A philosophy that excites the believer to sharpen his or her sickle and prepare for the greatest harvest ever reaped in all of history.
- A philosophy that believes the Church is a place of

growth, power and excitement; a place that God has ordained to become a force upon the earth. God is not pleased with evangelistic or missionary work that does not result in Church growth.

- A philosophy that propagates a positive approach to a negative society; a positive attitude of faith because the answer is found in Christ, and Christ is committed to the harvest.

- A philosophy that believes in the ultimate victory and triumph of the Church as God's last instrument to use in His eternal plan and purpose. This plan involves the house being filled with souls from all walks of life.

- A philosophy that believes that since God, as revealed in the Bible, has assigned the highest priority to bringing men into a living relationship with Jesus Christ, we may define our mission narrowly as an enterprise devoted to proclaiming the Good News of Jesus Christ and to persuading men to become His disciples and dependable members of His Church.

- A philosophy that sees the world as God's harvest field. Therefore, all unreached people groups in the world must be reached with the gospel of the Kingdom. A people have been reached only when many of its members have become disciples of Christ and responsible members of His Body. Until the Church is well rooted in that society, it has not been reached!

- A philosophy that clearly understands and honestly evaluates all growth by asking these questions: Is it biological growth? Is it transfer growth? Is it conversion growth?

- A philosophy that handles the tension of the discipling and perfecting debate. Usually antigrowth attitudes that hinder the harvesting vision and spirit within the Church arise from confusing "perfecting" with "discipling." The Church exists not for itself, but for the world. It always has a twofold task: winning people to Christ and maturing people in Christ (see Matt. 28:19,20).

- A philosophy that believes that as Christ's servants, we shall stand before His throne eternally saved, but nonetheless accountable to answer for our stewardship of the gospel entrusted to us and the souls committed to our care and dependent upon our witness.

- A philosophy that believes that at Christ's second coming and the resurrection of the dead, each human being shall be committed to either heaven or hell dependent upon his or her reception or rejection of Jesus Christ.

12. THE STONE OF REACHING CITIES FOR CHRIST

An article in issue 23 of *Christian History* magazine about the First Great Awakening describes the impact of that revival upon Jonathan Edwards's town. In Edwards's own words:

The work of God: As the number of true saints multiplied, it soon made a glorious alteration in the town, so that in the spring and summer following, anno 1735, the town seemed to be full of the presence of God; it was never so full of love, nor of joy, and yet so full of distress, as it was then. There were remarkable tokens of God's presence in almost every house. It was a time of joy in families on account of salvation being brought unto them. More than three hundred souls were sovereignly brought home to Christ, in this town, in the space of half a year.

The First Great Awakening penetrated towns, villages and larger cities, changing the way people lived, worked and experienced church life. Today, in the midst of revival trickles, we are praying and hoping with vision of our cities being penetrated by the power of the Holy Spirit. City reaching has taken on a new force among thousands of pastors, leaders and churches. Several influential leaders have been at the forefront of this truth. John Dawson and Ed Silvoso are two key strategists who have raised the water level on city reaching. John Dawson's book *Taking Our Cities for God* is one of the breakthrough books on this subject. Dawson speaks with boldness and insight about reaching cities:

> It is a sad but undeniable fact that too many of us in the Church have been so charmed by the intellectualism of culture that we have supposed our strength may be in matching its materialistic lines of reasoning. Consequently, much of the Church has been shorn of its power in dealing with the invisible realm and thereby crippled for making grand and sweeping breakthroughs in the arenas of deepest bondage and need—the world's cities. Like Samson, so many of us are bereft of power, shorn of its source, and blind to the reality of the invisible. Thus we 'grind at the mill,' plodding in circles like oxen, rather than moving ahead in spiritual power as sons and daughters of the Most High.[16]

The Church today indeed is floundering in the area of affecting whole cities for Christ, but change is coming. The Holy Spirit has raised up some men and women of God who are blowing their trumpets. Faith is being imparted to see entire cities and regions turn to Christ.

When I first began thinking about leading a whole city, I had not heard or read much about the concept. It was about 1980-82, and my wife and I were planting a church in Eugene, Oregon, where we were in the process of raising up a local church that would impact the city. I had very little training in the area of city strongholds, city personalities, city history, and spiritually mapping a city. None of these strategies were prominent 15 years ago. Now more and more material is being written. Cities are being impacted today, whole communities changed by the power of the gospel. George Otis, Jr.'s new book *Informed Intercession*, a guidebook on spiritual mapping and community transformation, lays out Kingdom principles that have not been widely exposed before now. Otis's research reveals the fact that transformed communities can happen!:

For some time now we have been hearing reports of large-scale conversions in places like China, Argentina and Nepal. In many instances, widespread healings, dreams and deliverances have attended these conversions. Confronted with these demonstrations of divine power and concern, multiplied thousands of men and women have elected to embrace the truth of the gospel. In a growing number of towns and cities, God's house is suddenly the place to be.[17]

Ed Silvoso agrees:

The word is becoming clearer and clearer. The Holy Spirit is saying to the churches: Take the cities for God and bring them into My Kingdom. I believe the primary target for God's spiritual armies in the 1990s is the cities of the world, not that other evangelistic targets are passé and unimportant. We must continue our aggressive effort to evangelize nations and people groups and individuals and religious and rural populations, reaching unsaved souls wherever they may be found. But let's be clear: Nothing is more important in our day than reaching our cities.[18]

The stone in the rivers of revival that we must not be intimidated to pick up is this one. Take your city on as your responsibility, your challenge, your calling. Thousands of pastors, leaders and intercessors are becoming convinced that city reaching is indeed a spiritual reality. It will not be done easily or without casualties, work, prayer and warfare, but it can be done and will be done. (We will develop this stone more fully later in this book.)

River truths, or truths illuminated during revival seasons, must be carefully kept by the Spirit and not allowed to become more orthodoxy or dead letter. Scholarship must be balanced with spiritual life as truths are documented, articulated and passed on to other people, movements and coming generations.

These 12 stones of truth are only representative stones. We could discuss several other newly illuminated truths such as apostolic ministry, prophetic gifts and leaders, extended fasting, lay ministry, prayer walking, networking and cross-pollination. Some of these we will touch on as we develop our theme of reaching cities.

In the meantime, look for some river stones that you may want to lay down for the next generation and allow the river of God's presence, anointing and life to stir the waters that surround them so they will maintain their life-giving power.

Anointing
By Howard Rachinski

Anointing, fall on me.
Fresh anointing, fall on me

As I worship in Your presence;
As I bow down in holy reverence.
My desire is to see Your glory, Lord.
So anointing, fresh anointing fall on me.

I have tasted of your goodness and your mercy.
I have seen your faithfulness;
But my heart is longing for more.
Fill me with your holiness.

Purge me, Lord,
And sanctify this vessel;
Purified I want to be.
Holy fire burn away my weakness.
Let Your power flow through me.[19]

PERSONAL APPLICATION

1. Are you willing to pick up stones of truth that may be controversial, causing others to attack you? What would some of those stones be in your church or denomination?

2. Have you picked up the stone of reconciling the generations? Or have you thrown stones of judgment at this generation? Would a grunge kid find an authentic Christ by getting to know you? If not, how do you need to change?

3. What have you done with the stone of racial reconciliation? Are you reaching out to someone of another race on a personal level? If not, will you commit to reaching out for Christ's sake in your community? And if you do not live in an integrated community, will you be the one to change it?

4. God is calling His people to a holy passion for harvesting souls. What does your life—your checkbook, the way you spend your time, the way you raise your children, the way you set your goals—say about your passion for harvesting souls?

Notes

1. Leonard Sweet, *Eleven Genetic Gateways to Spiritual Awakening* (Nashville: Abingdon Press, 1998), p. 17.
2. Barna Research Paper, taken from a prepublished manuscript.
3. Source unknown.
4. C. Peter Wagner, *How to Have a Healing Ministry in Any Church* (Ventura, CA: Regal Books, 1988), p. 143.
5. John Dawson, *Healing America's Wounds* (Ventura, CA: Regal Books, 1994), p. 23.
6. Raleigh Washington and Glen Kehrem, *Breaking Strongholds* (Chicago: Moody Press, 1993), p. 11.
7. C. Peter Wagner, *Warfare Prayer* (Ventura, CA: Regal Books, 1992), pp. 16, 17.
8. Harold Caballeros, *The Transforming Power of Revival* (Buenos, Aires, Argentina: El Shaddai Ministries, 1998), p. 14.
9. Carlos Annacondia, *Listen to Me, Satan!* (Lake Mary, FL: Creation House, 1997), p. 45.
10. Timothy Davis, *Cleansing Streams* (Van Nuys, CA: Glory Communications International, 1995).
11. Neil Anderson, *The Bondage Breaker* (Eugene, OR: Harvest House, 1993), p. 13.
12. William Carey, source unknown.
13. George Whitefield, source unknown.
14. Henry Martyn, source unknown.
15. David Brainerd, source unknown.
16. John Dawson, *Taking Our Cities for God* (Lake Mary, FL: Creation House, 1989), p. 12.

17. George Otis, Jr., *Informed Intercession* (Ventura, CA: Regal Books, 1999), prepublication manuscript.
18. Ed Silvoso, *That None Should Perish* (Ventura, CA: Regal Books, 1994), p. 9.
19. Howard Rachinski, "Anointing," City Bible Music, 1998. Used with permission.

CHAPTER 6

THE
GILGAL PRINCIPLE
AND POWER

*Then the Lord said to Joshua, "This day I have rolled
away the reproach of Egypt from you." Therefore the
name of the place is called Gilgal to this day.*

JOSHUA 5:9

The crossing of the Jordan was, up to this point, the single most
significant event in the life of the Israelites. To be brought out of
Egypt was one thing, but to now cross over this Jordan River and
be committed to whatever lay ahead without possibility of
retreat was another reality to be faced. Israel was now committed
to confronting the powers of Canaan. No more talking about it.
No more prayers for the coming warfare in the future. It was
now reality. They were in the land of warfare.

The river crossing was a high time for the Israelites—rejoicing,
celebrating, sensing God's supernatural hand upon them and

anticipating a great future. But slowly the reality of where they were began to sink in—the impregnable cities of Canaan, chariots of iron, the large and world-renowned armies, the 10 voices of the spies who predicted defeat. All this was sinking into the hearts of the people. They had come to the place of no return, no retreat and no compromise. Everything was on the line. They risked either gaining a miraculous future or losing everything. They had carried the 12 stones out as a memorial, a memory of the absolute power of a living God who works for His people at all times (see Josh. 4:19-24). Those stones would be needed now. They had to believe in that same power to root out the Caananite forces and to establish the purposes of God.

This is precisely the journey we take when we are determined to reach our cities for Christ. The crossing of revival rivers, the gathering of revival truths, the celebrating of revival power—all are glorious. In these moments, the power and presence of God is so real, so powerful and so inspirational. In these prophetic moments, we write out great visions; we proclaim awesome missions statements; we preach, teach and prophesy victory over and destruction of our enemies. Demons will flee, strongholds will be torn down and our cities will be taken.

THE RIVER CLOSES BEHIND ISRAEL— NO TURNING BACK

As we enjoy these precious moments of God's visitation, the river is slowly closing. The passageway for retreat is shut. Our future is sealed, and little do we know what is in store for us.

The river miracle was not just to inspire the people of God but, in God's own unique way, to trap the people so they could not turn back. In the near future, they would face 30 different hostile armies and fight 3 long military campaigns. They would learn how to take each city by God's wisdom with a custom-made plan for each city. Many would lose their lives in the battles to come. In the end, the people of God would overcome and inherit the cities and settle the land, but not without paying a dear price.

At first you map the city, strategize and prepare. Later the demonic forces map you, strategize against your every step and make pans to destroy your city-reaching vision and spirit.

Such is the nature of city reaching. It begins with worship but moves quickly to warfare. What begins with power and presence proceeds quickly to pain and pressure. I hope my application here does not disturb or defeat your enthusiasm about reaching your city, region, state or nation. The journey we have embarked upon has proven Joshua's teachings for us to be accurate and our steps into it to be careful. What may inspire you about city reaching must also prepare you for confronting the powers of hell.

At first you map the city, strategize and prepare. Later the demonic forces map you, strategize against your every step and make plans to destroy your city-reaching vision and spirit. The good news is that God is more powerful and wise than all the demonic forces. The bad news is that the river has just closed behind you, and there is no turning back.

Gilgal, the Prelude to Reaching Jericho

The Israelites had crossed over the river (see Josh. 4:19-24; 5:9,10). They had also crossed over the dividing line and now entered a new day, a new way of doing things. Canaan represents a new kind of warfare, a new style of leadership, a new way of receiving God's provision. Their first stop is Gilgal, a transition point, a place of God cutting away the past. Gilgal was strategically located. The Jordan provided security on the one side and the open plain prevented surprise attacks from the other side. They had all the water they needed and a place to stop so they could wait upon the Lord and prepare for their first city-reaching operation—Jericho. Before they moved into direct confrontation with Canaanite powers, the Israelites must first receive personal deliverance—circumcision, the cutting away of the old.

Gilgal means rolling away. Here it indicates the rolling away of the reproach of Egypt:

> So it was, when all the kings of the Amorites who were on the west side of the Jordan, and all the kings of the Canaanites who were by the sea, heard that the LORD had dried up the waters of the Jordan from before the children of Israel until we had crossed over, that their heart melted; and there was no spirit in them any longer because of the children of Israel. At that time the LORD said to Joshua, "Make flint knives for yourself, and circumcise the sons of Israel again the second time." So Joshua made flint knives for himself, and circumcised the sons of Israel at the hill of the foreskins. And this is the reason why Joshua circumcised them: All the people who came out of Egypt who were males, all the men of war, had died in the wilderness on the way, after they had come out of

Egypt. For all the people who came out had been circumcised, but all the people born in the wilderness, on the
way as they came out of Egypt, had not been circumcised.
For the children of Israel walked forty years in the
wilderness, till all the people who were men of war, who
came out of Egypt, were consumed, because they did not
obey the voice of the LORD—to whom the LORD swore
that He would not show them the land which the LORD
had sworn to their fathers that He would give us, "a land
flowing with milk and honey." Then Joshua circumcised
their sons whom He raised up in their place; for they were
uncircumcised, because they had not been circumcised on
the way. So it was, when they had finished circumcising
all the people, that they stayed in their places in the
camp till they were healed. Then the LORD said to
Joshua, "This day I have rolled away the reproach of
Egypt from you." Therefore the name of the place is
called Gilgal to this day (Josh. 5:1-9).

THE CUTTING AWAY

Circumcision is the seal of the covenant between God and
Abraham and all his descendants (see Gen. 17:9-14). This act of
circumcising a new generation was the rejoining of this generation to the covenant purposes of God. The sons of Israel were to
carry in their very person this mark of separateness. Even as this
outward sign of circumcision was to mirror an inward work of
God in their hearts (see Deut. 10:16; 30:6), so we too must have
the inward mark of separateness in our hearts (see Col. 2:11-13).

God's way is the way of humiliation. Our life of circumcision
is a life where the natural, carnal man is cut away. At the place of
our natural power and our natural ability, God desires a total

dedication to Himself. The land set before us will not be taken by any natural strength or carnal power. It will only be given to those who have learned that the secret power of God lies with the brokenhearted, those who are contrite in spirit. Gilgal becomes the base of operations for Israel's military career as Gilgal becomes the base of our operation for reaching cities.

Jordan was not enough. Gilgal must be experienced as we approach our Jericho. First a separation, then a rejoining to God as a covenant God, reuniting with His covenantal purposes to reach all people with the gospel. Gilgal is symbolic of revival people going to a deeper level of commitment and to a deeper level of personal preparation. Gilgal is symbolic of entering into a new place of fellowship with the Lord, a new obedience to His every word, and a new sensitivity to His every command.

We cannot reach cities until we first receive new hearts and roll away our Egyptian-based strategies and Egyptian mind-sets on how to accomplish great things for our God. Moses was learned in all the ways of Egypt, but he used none of them. The wilderness is the stripping of our natural strength. Gilgal is the sealing of this by allowing God to cut away, not just the actions that are wrong, but our heart motivations. Gilgal is the place of change. It is where we place our 12 revival stones to remember God's power and develop newfound truths. These 12 truths are for the future. They are part of city reality. Gilgal is the place to circumcise the hearts of God's people, to roll away our past and to allow God to provide for us a new strategy.

THE MARK OF A NEW BEGINNING AND NEW PROVISIONS

Gilgal is the place of our first Passover in the land. It signifies that our cities will not be reached without the power of the Lamb of God, the power of the blood of sacrifice and the fellowship of God's people around Jesus rather than dogmas, doctrines and creeds:

> Now the children of Israel camped in Gilgal, and kept the Passover on the fourteenth day of the month at twilight on the plains of Jericho. And they ate of the produce of the land on the day after the Passover, unleavened bread and parched grain, on the very same day. Then the manna ceased on the day after they had eaten the produce of the land; and the children of Israel no longer had manna, but they ate the food of the land of Canaan that year (Josh. 5:10-12).

The Passover would assure them that He who had been with them in the Exodus would sustain and protect them now. The circumcision would remind them of God's promise; the Passover would remind them of His power to deliver—and the two together would lead them to encourage themselves in the Lord their God.

Gilgal is the place where the manna ceases and we partake of the produce of the land. The rich produce of Canaan—of our cities and nations—is set aside for those who cross over the Jordan rivers and prepare properly at Gilgal. Deuteronomy 28 relates the principle by which God worked with Israel: Obedience brings blessing; disobedience brings chastisement. That principle is operative in Joshua 5:11,12. Following Israel's obedience in practicing circumcision and in keeping the memorial of Passover, God blessed the nation by giving the Israelites the firstfruits of the land. On the day following the Passover, Israel ate some of the produce of the land. This was God's down payment to Israel, indicating that He was giving them the land (see Lev. 23:5-14).

The New Captain

Before Joshua proceeds to his first city-reaching challenge, he encounters the true leader of Israel's armies, the Captain of the Lord of Hosts:

> And it came to pass, when Joshua was by Jericho, that he lifted his eyes and looked, and behold, a Man stood opposite him with His sword drawn in His hand. And Joshua went to Him and said to Him, "Are You for us or for our adversaries?" So He said, "No, but as Commander of the army of the LORD I have now come." And Joshua fell on his face to the earth and worshiped, and said to Him, "What does my Lord say to His servant?" Then the Commander of the LORD's army said to Joshua, "Take your sandal off your foot, for the place where you stand is holy." And Joshua did so (Josh. 5:13-15).

Joshua was surveying the city. He did not know the exact intentions of Jehovah in approaching this great walled city. Suddenly, as Joshua lifted his eyes, an armed man was seen standing over him. Joshua's question was certainly the right question concerning the circumstance. "Are you for us or for our enemies?"

The Man responded, "Neither. I come as the commander of the army of the Lord." Commander signifies a military leader, a general. It is the same term used in the phrase "Prince of Peace" in Isaiah 9:6. This unnamed general identified himself as commander over the armies of the Lord, obviously both in heaven and earth. The concept is similar to that presented in 1 Kings 22:19 when the prophet Micaiah saw the "host of heaven" attending the Lord who was seated on His throne. Thus, the army of the Lord in Joshua 5:14 designates the angels of heaven (see Pss. 103:21; 148:2), but more particularly in warfare for the Lord.

When Joshua realized whom he was facing, he fell on his face and worshiped God! City reaching always begins with an encounter with the real Captain of the army. The Church is under His command. As we go into warfare, it is encouraging to realize that Jesus has His sword drawn. He is not only leading the attack to take our Jericho, but He is also vitally involved in every way. He proclaims His authority: "As Captain I come." This is absolute authority over all the affairs of humanity and all the evil forces to be encountered.

The appearance of the unnamed Man is best understood as a theophany, a manifestation of Christ in the Old Testament. A theophany usually took the form of an angel or a man and is most frequently designated in the Old Testament as the "angel of the Lord" (see Gen. 16:7-13; 21:17; 22:11; 48:15,16; Exod. 3:2; Judg. 6:11-24). Joshua submits to this Commander, recognizing Him to be the Lord in charge of all city-taking campaigns.

The stage is now set for God to direct Joshua in a very surprising and unique method for city reaching. It is not the plan anyone had in mind. This is not the type of warfare the enemy expected or that Israel anticipated. God's ways are so much higher and so opposite to our ways (see Isa. 55:9-11). Joshua had yielded his agenda to the Captain of the Lord of Hosts. He was positioned to hear and obey.

City reaching can only be successful when the Captain of heaven is directing His people with heavenly plans and heavenly power. The fact that in many cities there are numerous different, unfruitful plans in operation makes one suspect that the Captain of the Lord's armies may not be directing all this activity on earth. The first step toward city ministry is some level of

City Church submission and obedience to the Lord of Hosts. After all, there is really only one Church in every city and one Lord who is Chief Commander.

You are not ready for war until you have

been saturated by the presence of the

Lord of Hosts.

Before the Captain of the Lord of Hosts began to give the battle strategy, he told Joshua to take off his shoes. When God asks leaders to take off their shoes, He certainly is not expecting them to move out very quickly. A person without shoes is expected to stay a while. With the resurgence of prayer and fasting in the Church today, I believe many leaders will hear a voice saying, "Remove your shoes." You are not ready for war until you have been saturated by the presence of the Lord of Hosts.

Maybe our first step toward taking our Jericho could be to stop, bow and worship, to take off our shoes and realize the battle is the Lord's. Joshua was receiving the Lord's approval for his city-reaching leadership; as God revealed Himself to Moses, so now to Moses' successor. Amid a land defiled by an idolatrous people, the place where the Lord stood became a holy place, sanctified because of His presence.

This encounter with the new Captain was strategically important for Joshua, a man of war. He was to submit totally and unconditionally to the Lord of Hosts, the Heavenly Captain—all the plans, strategies, methods, leaders to be chosen, armies to be sent, the timing, number of soldiers to be recruited and the approaches to take to each opposing force—all had to be submitted.

Joshua 5:14 records the foundational attitude for city-reaching leadership: "What does my Lord say to His servant?" This need for complete openness is a hindrance to most leaders because most things that come from above are not always pleasing to man's natural, carnal mind. We would rather reason, argue our points of truth and excuse unnatural means as unfruitful, even to the point of calling certain things erroneous, heresy, cultish or religious stupidity.

The leader who follows the Lord's directions, fulfilling all He says with prompt obedience, will be faced with criticism and ridicule. The symbolic acts of the prophets will shed some light on how God asks His people to do the ridiculous that He might do the miraculous.

THE SYMBOLIC ACTS OF THE PROPHETS

The following are instances in which a prophet of God performed an action that represented a spiritual truth to the hearers:[1]

1. Jeremiah wore a yoke around his neck through the streets to depict the impending Babylonian bondage (see Jer. 27,28).
2. Hosea was commanded to marry a harlot, symbolizing Israel's unfaithfulness (see Hosea 1—3).
3. Isaiah walked naked and barefoot for three years, symbolizing that Egypt and Ethiopia were at the hands of Assyria (see Isa. 20:1-6).
4. Ezekiel was commanded to lay mock siege to Jerusalem by portraying it upon a tile (see Ezek. 4:1-3).
5. Ezekiel was commanded to lie on his left side for 390

days and upon his right side for 40 days. The number of days represented the number of years that Israel had disobeyed and forsaken God throughout its history (see Ezek. 4:4-8).

6. Ezekiel was commanded to eat different kinds of food for 390 days, symbolizing the ceremonial defilement that would come to the Israelites in being forced to partake of Gentile food during their captivity (see Ezek. 4:9-17).

7. Ezekiel was commanded to burn a portion of his hair, foretelling the coming destruction of Jerusalem and its inhabitants (see Ezek. 5:1-4).

8. Ezekiel was commanded to shave his hair and beard and scatter some of the hair, symbolizing the scattering of the Jews to various parts of the earth (see Ezek. 5:1-4).

9. Ezekiel was commanded to prophesy to a dry bone-yard, symbolizing Israel's spiritual dryness and death. This prophecy foretells the promised blessing upon Israel in and through the New Covenant (see Ezek. 37).

10. Ahizah, upon meeting Jeroboam, rent his garment in 12 pieces, symbolizing the division of his kingdom (see 1 Kings 11:30).

11. Jeremiah symbolically gave signs to Israel by:
    a. A marred girdle, symbolizing the negative effect the 70-year captivity in Babylon would have upon the house of Judah (see Jer. 13:1).
    b. A potter and the clay, speaking of the judgment of God coming to the house of Judah and the resulting blessing upon them in and through the New Covenant (see Jer. 18:1-6).
    c. A cup of the wine of wrath, speaking of the judgment of God being stored up for ungodly nations (see Jer. 25:15).

12. Certain prophets were commanded to give prophetic symbolic names to their children:
   a. Isaiah's children:
      · Shear-Jashub: "A remnant shall return" (see Isa. 7:3).
      · Maher-Shalah-Hash-Baz: "The spoil speeded, the prey hasteth" (see Isa. 8:1).
   b. Hosea's children:
      · Jezreel: "It will be sown in God" (Hos. 1:4).
      · Lo-Ruhamah: "No mercy" (v. 6).
      · Lo-Ammi: "Not my people" (v. 9).
13. Ezekiel was commanded to prophesy to the mountains. Mountains in Scripture represent various kingdoms and nations of the earth (see Ezek. 6:1-3).
14. Ezekiel was commanded to move by digging through a wall, representing Judah's being removed to Babylon (see Ezek. 12:1-6).
15. Jeremiah was commanded to buy a linen girdle, to put it on but not wash it, and then to go to the Euphrates and hide it there in a hole of the rock. Then he was commanded to dig it up, even though it was marred and good for nothing, symbolizing what God was going to do to the pride of Jerusalem and Judah (see Jer. 13:1-11).
16. Jeremiah was commanded to take an earthen vessel in front of the ancients of the people and the ancients of the priests, symbolizing the destruction of Jerusalem (see Jer. 19:1-9).
17. Ezekiel remained dumb for seven days after his call, representing his identification with the miseries and trials of those to whom he would minister (see Ezek. 3:15).
18. Agabus bound the apostle Paul with his girdle, symbolizing what the Jews were going to do to him in Jerusalem (see Acts 21:10-14).

What the Lord says to His servants may seem to be a simple key for city reaching, but will probably be a stretch for most of us. All divine revelation for twenty-first-century leaders lies in the direction of the unseen world. This is usually a point of contention for those trained in the basic American worldview, but not so in other parts of the world.

The unseen world is affected by interacting with the physical world, the tangible. City reaching involves the unseen, invisible world, and the world that must be invaded by a people who understand what to do. The Church must hear what the Spirit is saying, for in the Spirit are spiritual plans—strategies that are powerful and effective. The kingdom of God is in the Holy Spirit, and it is precisely in this realm of the Spirit that we will be successful.

Joshua models for all leaders and churches the basics of preparing to reach our cities for Christ. The enormity of the world calls for extraordinary commitment to Christ and His ways.

We live in a world of evil, corrupt principalities, and the mighty powers of darkness seek to possess our world. Our calling is to exterminate all evil powers that hold people, families, neighborhoods and cities in their wicked grip. This calling is for all believers; it is our Kingdom mandate to reach all people and all cities with the gospel (see 1 Tim. 2:4,5; 2 Pet. 3:9).

Ed Silvoso says, "Cities are central to God's redemptive strategy. The Great Commission begins with a city, Jerusalem, and culminates with another city, the New Jerusalem, which becomes God's eternal dwelling with His people. In order to fulfill the Great Commission, we must reach every city on earth with the gospel."[2]

With uncircumcised hearts and Egyptian mind-sets behind us, we will find ourselves ready to move from the place of receiving manna to becoming a source of broken bread for the hurting world around us—we learn this at Gilgal.

I Will Wait on the Lord
By Sharon Damazio

I will wait on the Lord;
I will listen to His voice.
Where He leads me I will follow;
I will wait on the Lord.
I will wait on the Lord.

Like an eagle in the sky,
I was meant to fly
And soar upon the wings of prayer and praise.
Learning to rest,
Learning to trust in the Lord
And follow all His ways.
There are times when I'm weary;
He will make me strong.
When the road is dark and lonely,
He is there to lead me home.[3]

PERSONAL APPLICATION

1. Have you, like the Israelites, received a life-changing promise that now seems to oppose you with a fear that the circumstances before you are too great to conquer? Has the river closed behind you? Can you now see that there is no turning back because God has brought you here?

2. Have you taken your shoes off, or are you still running to meet your Jericho in your own strength? Will you

bow to God's timing? Will you worship Him and recognize that the battle is the Lord's?

3. Circumcision is painful. It takes us out of commission for a time in order to heal. Where has God laid the blade of His sword of the Spirit on your flesh as you have sought your land of promise?

4. Are you willing to bear the humiliation of doing something that does not earn people's approval for the sake of the gospel? If you said yes, don't be surprised if your yes is put to the test.

Notes

1. Frank Damazio, *Developing the Prophetic Ministry* (Portland, OR: BT Publishing, 1983), pp. 19-21.
2. Ed Silvoso, *That None Should Perish* (Ventura, CA: Regal Books, 1994), p. 21.
3. Sharon Damazio, "I Will Wait on the Lord," City Bible Music, 1998. Used with permission.

APPROACHING OUR

JERICHO: WHY THE CITY IS SECURELY SHUT UP

Now Jericho was securely shut up because of the children of Israel; none went out, and none came in.

JOSHUA 6:1

We now turn our attention to God's plan for reaching our cities with the gospel of the Kingdom. To reach a city for Christ, necessary foundation stones must be set in place. The Joshua Model had yielded several pertinent facts for preparing a people to take the land, to reach the cities and to establish new Kingdom power where alien, evil powers had previously ruled.

The following are lessons from the Joshua Model:

• To be a vanguard, one must advance into the future, taking from the past what is spiritually applicable for all generations and leaving behind those things that have already become obsolete.

- We are crossing over a new river and entering into a new era, a new culture, a new, modern, secular world, a post-Christian generation, a time when leaders cannot do business as usual.

- We must choose to enter into the rivers of revival around us in this present day, rivers of Holy Spirit activity caused by seasonal outpourings of the presence of God upon hungry hearts, resulting in cleansing, new passion, new vision and a new day.

- The headwaters of revival have three distinct levels of flowing water before the river level is reached. Rills are tiny narrow channels of water that multiply and form wider deeper channels called brooks. And brooks again merge with other brooks, gaining momentum and depth that eventually become streams, which are more permanent and grow larger. Rills, brooks and streams are the tributaries that create rivers. First the natural, then the spiritual.

- We must prepare for each revival river by embracing the truth of personal holiness—our Acacia Grove experience—before crossing the river. This fresh and life-changing encounter with biblical holiness assures a longevity of Holy Spirit activity.

- As we prepare to enter revival rivers, we are to dip our feet into the waters and allow the river to soak us and add to us. Every revival river has truth that must be discovered and assimilated; yet every church and movement of churches should build upon its previously established biblical distinctives. Revival truths should add to, not take away from.

- We need to discover the river stones in revival rivers, define those stones of truth, lift them out of the river and carry them over to the other side. These stones become directional stones for the next generation, stones we ' build altars with, altars of dedication and destiny.
- We must embrace the truth that churches are called to reach whole cities for Christ, to develop God-given strategies that will result in destroying satanic strongholds in the city and powerfully impact every person, every household, every neighborhood with the gospel of salvation until the city is reached for Christ.

Building upon these foundational city-reaching truths discovered in Joshua chapters 1—5, we now move into Joshua 6, the first city-reaching encounter for Joshua and a city-reaching school for us.

CITY-REACHING STRATEGIES 101

Now Jericho was securely shut up because of the children of Israel; none went out, and none came in. And the Lord said to Joshua: "See! I have given Jericho into your hand, its king, and the mighty men of valor" (Josh. 6:1,2).

The strategy that would be employed by Joshua to reach all of Canaan was given to Joshua in stages—one situation at a time. The strategy would involve three main phases—three main military campaigns—beginning with the central campaign, then moving to the southern campaign, and finally ending with the northern campaign.

The first city encounter was to be Jericho, a very strategic city to the whole of Canaan. By entering the land at Jericho, the land would be divided in half, prohibiting any significant alliances between the northern and southern city-states. This strategy was given by the Captain of the Lord of Hosts. He really does have a fuller view of city reaching; He can see the whole plan.

This first conflict is a firstfruits conflict—what is accomplished here has far-reaching ramifications for the taking of all other cities. In this first city-reaching experience, God would leave nothing to human reasoning or human discretion. God would have no hesitation before the enemy; every movement would be firm and measured. The strategic plan for this first battle was given as an aid to faith in all battles to come.

As Joshua prepared to take his first city, you can be sure there was no small amount of fear and talk of retreat. The two factors that kept the people in place and moving forward were (1) the river had shut behind them, and (2) they had rehearsed the vision, the great rewards that lay in their future upon taking the land. Canaan was a land of milk and honey, a good land and a large land (see Exod. 3:8), a land of corn and wine and kissed with the dews of heaven (see Deut. 33:28), a land of olives and vines, of firs and cedars, of rich fruits and harvest where an obedient people should eat to the full, where the threshing should reach unto the vintage and the vintage unto the sowing time (see Lev. 26:5). The land was described in detail by Moses in Deuteronomy 6:10-12, an awesome vision for the people:

> Which He swore to your fathers, to Abraham, Isaac, and Jacob, to give you large and beautiful cities which you did not build, houses full of all good things, which you did not fill, hewn-out wells which you did not dig, vineyards and olive trees which you did not plant—when you have eaten and are full—then beware, lest you forget the LORD who brought you out of the land of Egypt, from the house of bondage (Deut. 6:10-12).

Before possessing this awesome land there would be warfare—challenges beyond their abilities and strengths. As the Israelites stood in front of the first city, the entry point, the beginning of possessing their future, their destiny was at stake. Jericho. Why did the hardest city have to be the "entry point" city? So they would learn that the God they served was greater than all the gods they would meet in combat. No city was strong enough to resist the power and wisdom of the true living God (see Deut. 9:1-6; 12:29; 18:9-14; Josh. 5:13-15).

A CURE FOR SICK CITIES

Today's cities engage in spiritual warfare daily for the soul of the city. Today's cities are by nature apostate corporations. Even the best accomplishments bear the marks of sinful and active hostility against God and His Word. Today's cities are steeped in modern-day deceptions. Humanistic idealists are supported by enlightened planning with dedicated leaders who promise a cure for all city ills through greater dedicated efforts and modern technology. This, of course, isn't working and won't work. Our cities are sick, and the only hope for a cure is a miraculous heart transplant—one that can only happen by the preaching of the gospel.

Joshua 6:1 reads, "Now Jericho was securely shut up because of the children of Israel. None went out and none came in." The book *26 Translations of the Old Testament* translates the phrase "securely shut up" as being "carefully barricaded against the Israelites, bolted and barred, shut up from within and without, and closed in and secured."[1]

Jericho's defense was formidable. The walls were a type that made direct assault practically impossible. An approaching army first encountered a stone abutment, 11 feet high, back and up from which sloped a 35-degree, plastered scarp reaching to the main wall some 35 feet above. The steep, smooth slope prohibited battering the wall by any effective device or building fires to break it. An army trying to storm the wall found difficulty in climbing the slope, and ladders used to scale it could find no satisfactory footing. The normal tactics used by an enemy to take a city would not work if Israel was to occupy all the land in any reasonable number of months.[2]

Tracing City Roots to Break Satanic Strongholds

The first step to city reaching is understanding how our cities are securely shut up from within and without. We must see our cities and regions as they really are, not merely as they appear to be. More than 42 cities in the world have a population of more than 4 million people; most are Asian or Islamic. In the United States of America, large cities are inhabited by different races of people, making the United States one of the major mission fields of the world. The statistics for Los Angeles alone are quite enlightening:

- 4.5 million Hispanics;
- Second largest Chinese city outside China;
- Second largest Japanese city outside Japan;
- Largest Korean city outside Korea;
- Largest Vietnamese city outside Vietnam;
- Largest Philippine city outside the Philippines.

Our vision for missions must focus on cities. God's plan begins in the garden, but ends in the city. God has vision for our cities. Our cities can become places of shelter, communion, purity and hope. Our cities have been marked by God's sovereign plan and purpose; our responsibility is to discover and to release

God's plan in our cities. Arnold Toynbee states in his book *Cities of Destiny*, "In order to become a city, it would have to evolve at least the rudiments of a soul. This is perhaps the essence of cityhood."[3] The soul of your city must be discerned.

God's plan begins in the garden, but ends in the city. Our responsibility is to discover and to release God's plan in our cities.

In *Commitment to Conquer*, Bob Beckett encourages every leader and church congregation to understand its community, not just what appears to be the community chemistry, but the real personality of the community. Beckett says, "To understand a community, we must first understand that every city, like every individual, is unique. No two cities are exactly the same. We may find similarities in traits, appearance, even to some extent history, but the fact remains that there is no other city like your city; God's plan for each city is unique. Satan's strategy to hold a city in bondage is also unique to every situation, and generally in direct contrast to God's plan. Here is where spiritual mapping enters the picture. It is through the methods and practices of spiritual mapping that we come to understand our communities and how best to minister to them."[4]

George Otis, Jr., one of the world's foremost leaders in spiritual mapping and transforming communities, defines the basics of spiritual mapping: "The discipline of spiritual mapping offers one of the best means of enhancing our perspective on reality. Unlike conventional interpretive devices, spiritual mapping does not confine itself to a single dimension. Rather it works by superimposing our understanding of forces and events in the spiritual domain into places and circumstances in the material world."[5]

ASKING THE RIGHT QUESTIONS

When I first began a serious journey into reaching our city, I realized I didn't understand my own city or region. Spiritual mapping was a new buzzword I had heard about and simply dismissed as not being the kind of ministry I would be interested in. I thought it sounded too subjective, unreal and over-spiritualizing of simple obvious matters within cities. But as we pursued a strategy to become more effective as a church in ministering to our city, we needed more information regarding the whys of our own city. They included:

- Why do we have certain obvious black holes in our city/region?
- Why do we draw New Age followers?
- Why were we the first state to pass a legalized suicide bill?
- Why do we lead the nation in pornography stores per capita?

These questions led us on a quest to study our history, our moral climate and the reason certain areas in our city have been untouched by the gospel for more than 100 years.

Spiritual mapping is one term used to describe a process by which churches accumulate researched information to better aid prayer intercession and targeted areas of ministry. Why is your city securely shut up? What are the forces that hold the city in spiritual poverty and spiritual bondage?

A LOOK AT GUATEMALA'S ROOTS

Harold Caballeros is pastor of El Shaddai Church in Guatemala City and a leader in spiritual mapping, spiritual warfare and transforming communities through intercessory prayer. He describes his journey as beginning with unveiling the hidden forces behind the bondages in his own community:

It was 1990 when El Shaddai Church dedicated our new property to the Lord and everything seemed like a celebration. I never imagined that a small earth mound on the back of the property would unchain a series of events that would profoundly impact our ministry. Due to a legal problem related to land leveling, we discovered that this mound was not just a bunch of dirt, it was a national monument. We were completely amazed to find out that this monument is the "Grand Snake Mound of the Valley of Guatemala."

When we researched this, our surprise was even greater. The measurements of this monument, built by hand more than 200 years before Christ, was 30 meters wide, 15 meters high and 21 kilometers long. Can you imagine a handmade snake of that size? Why would someone want to build such a monument? Trying to find the answer to this question, we became acquainted with the god worshiped by the first inhabitants of what we know today as the Valley of Guatemala. His name was Quetzalcoatl, the feathered snake. Our research yielded unexpected results. Our country had been offered and dedicated to this principality. What we discovered after this was even more revealing: this god's features were reflected in all of our society.

This is how we discovered the principle stated by the apostle Paul in chapter one of the book of Romans: we can perceive the invisible through the visible things. We began to see that the physical, natural realm was a reflection of the invisible spiritual powers that had originated in what is seen. Little by little we became aware that the root of all the problems that plagued our country coincided exactly with the "pacts" made between the early inhabitants of the land and the powers they worshiped.[6]

INFORMED INTERCESSION

This kind of discovery is simply what George Otis, Jr. calls "informed intercession." The more we become aware of the historical and spiritual root systems, pacts made, gods worshiped, and driving forces behind evil, the more we can smart bomb our adversary through informed prayer intercession. God is calling His Church to disciple cities, reaching them through informed intercession and servant leaders who network together to accomplish the task.

Spiritual darkness is increasing, not decreasing, so the Church must increase in power and discernment. Darkness through various demonic forces is on the increase in our world; behind the visible is the invisible. We need to know what evil forces are driving our legislative and judicial systems into legalizing rights of pressure groups, no matter how damaging these causes might be to society as a whole: exaggerated animal rights, gay rights, environmental trivia, abortion for convenience, euthanasia and moral perversion. All are growing more intense and more blatantly against God, His Word and His Church.

If the Church had all the power and wisdom to stop this evil landslide in days past, why didn't we do it? It could be that we have been fighting a high-tech battle with a typewriter mentality! We need to upgrade our weapons of war and our strategies to use them. Spiritual darkness is increasing and is becoming more sophisticated. There is a geographical pattern to evil and oppression in our cities; we need to accept that and discern where this pattern is unbroken. Most people do not understand the spiritual dimension as well as they thought; we need an upgrade and we need it now.

VICTORY COMES NOT BY MAN'S MIGHT BUT BY GOD'S POWER

The word to Joshua is based on facts: The city is securely shut up; there is no way to penetrate this city unless you follow the instructions of the Captain of the Lord of Hosts. This word is for Joshua leadership who will pay the price of preparation and follow God's strategy. Joshua 6:2 says, "And the Lord said to Joshua, 'See! I have given Jericho into your hand, its king, and the mighty men of valor.'"

*Massive intellects, strong wills and hardened
hearts cannot hope to resist strongholds
destroyed by prayer intercession.*

The cities of the twenty-first century need missionaries, visionaries with a Joshua word—the city is already given into your hand. Even though our cities have been shut up with iron gates and strengthened with bars of brass, God has decreed He will penetrate each and every city. The efforts of the invisible world to resist God are weak and foolish; they will give way to a Holy Spirit-penetrating Church. Iron, brass and stone for gates and walls are as nothing in the hands of Him who made them. Massive intellects, strong wills and hardened hearts cannot hope to resist strongholds destroyed by prayer intercession.

The closed and barred Jericho is an image of closed and barred people, homes and cities. The victory is sure, it will be complete, and it may be sudden. The Commander of the Lord's army was promising Joshua the down payment for Israel's appropriation of the land. God was giving the Israelites the city. It would not be taken by the ingenuity of men, but by the power of God. The city has already been defeated in God's eyes:

> Give us help from trouble, for vain is the help of man. Through God we will do valiantly, for it is He who shall tread down our enemies (Ps. 108:12,13).

Moreover, the tense of the verb phrase "I have delivered" indicates that the battle has already been won, as previously stated by Rahab to the 12 spies in Joshua 2:8-11:

> Now before they lay down, she came up to them on the roof, and said to the men: "I know that the LORD has given you the land, that the terror of you has fallen on us, and that all the inhabitants of the land are faint-hearted because of you. For we have heard how the LORD dried up the water of the Red Sea for you when you came out of Egypt, and what you did to the two kings of the Amorites who were on the other side of the Jordan, Sihon and Og, whom you utterly destroyed. And as soon as we heard these things, our hearts melted; neither did

there remain any more courage in anyone because of you, for the LORD your God, He is God in heaven above and on earth beneath" (Josh. 2:8-11).

Expositor's Bible Commentary states that the conquest of a walled city was a major challenge. Yadin has listed five ways that a walled city could be captured:

1. By going over the wall using ladders, ramps, etc.;
2. By digging a tunnel under the wall;
3. By smashing a hole through the wall;
4. By laying siege until the city is starved into submission;
5. By some sort of subterfuge, i.e., the use of a wooden horse by the Greeks to conquer Troy and the use of ambush and decoy by the Israelites in capturing Ai (see Josh. 8:1-23).

The Israelites had not encountered walled cities prior to this, and after many years of wandering in the desert, they were not equipped for such an undertaking. High walls had discouraged the spies 40 years earlier (see Num. 13:28). The city of Jericho was strategically located as an imposing fortress guarding the fords across the Jordan and the passes into the hill country.

Our twenty-first-century cities certainly are high-walled fortresses that intimidate leaders worldwide. The complexity of the moral and social issues are enough to turn any pastor or spiritual leader's eyes toward the more simple surroundings of country churches, villages and towns. Who really wants to face the mighty warriors of the invisible world, the principalities that rule and reign over our cities? Nevertheless, the call to take cities is being heard by many leaders and faithful intercessors. In view of the rapid growth of cities in Asia, Africa and Latin America and the internationalization of cities in Europe and North American, it is no exaggeration to call cities the new frontier of Christian missions. For, like the world at large, missions tomorrow will be mostly urban. Christ calls the Church to bring the gospel not only to tribes and villages, but also to modern, socially complex centers of population, culture and political power.

TAKING OUR JERICHO

As we prepared for our first steps toward taking our Jericho, these words spoken to Joshua became my meat to do the Father's will. In the months and years to come, we would stumble and grope in darkness, searching for the right tools, the right ways, the right attitudes and the right timing. We would learn how to network with the greater Church of our region to accomplish this vision, reaching our metro area with the message of the kingdom of God. We would learn how much we didn't know, how little power we had against ruling forces over our metro area, and how unprepared we were for counterattacks. We would learn the words "commitment," "perseverance," "pacing," "prayer," "patience" and "humility." We would learn more about our metro areas than we ever thought possible or necessary. The city is securely shut up and the Lord has already given it unto our hands, yet we face a king and his mighty warriors. We accumulated research on our Jericho and began our city-reaching journey. Our research yielded information absolutely necessary for ministry to our city.

OUR REGION'S HISTORY

Portland, Oregon, and Vancouver, Washington, which make up our greater metropolitan area, were first inhabited by Chinook Indians with seven dialects dividing them into seven tribes:

Cathaporte, Clackamas, Clowewalla, Klickitat, Multnomah, Skiloot and Tualatin. The first white settlers arrived in 1825, sent by the British Hudson's Bay Company to build and operate Fort Vancouver. Portland's first name was "The Clearing," and it was purchased by two men, F. W. Pettigrove and Lawrence Lovejoy. Pettigrove was from Maine and wanted to name the city Portland, but Lovejoy was from Massachusetts and wanted to name it Boston. They flipped a coin, and from 1845 until now, the city has been called Portland. From its very beginning, the Portland-Vancouver area had three main obvious problems:

1. **Political Corruption.** Mr. Wheelwright, the president of the Portland Chamber of Commerce in 1905, stated, "We are witnesses to a spectacle of public and private rottenness that is almost precedent in the annals of the country." Mr. Feney, the U.S. Prosecutor in 1905, stated, "You men corrupt everything you touch."

2. **Blatant Vice in the North End.** From 1860 until this present day, Burnside Street has been a significant boundary in Portland. North of Burnside, we have had junkies, hobos, gamblers, vagrants, prostitutes, scavengers, criminals, gangs and more for at least 138 years. In 1860, a group called "The Puritan Soldiers of the Lord" opposed the adversary, "Satan's City." Satan's City was the nickname of the north end with its alcohol, drugs, sex and poverty. The area was also called "The City of Destruction" because it destroyed any soul that went into it.

3. **Racial Prejudice.** The Portland metro area is home to about 85 percent white and 15 percent all other races. This is the highest percentage of Caucasians among the 50 largest cities in America. African-American is

8 percent, Asian 5 percent and Native American 1 percent. Though the African-Americans are a small minority, they have suffered considerable hostility. In 1884, the first exclusion law passed requiring all blacks to leave Oregon within three years or be subject to violent public whippings. In 1957, more exclusion laws were passed; Oregon was to remain a removed Eden dedicated to the destinies of white people only. The greatest racial injustice was against the Native Americans, reducing them to a mere shadow by 1880. Only 20 years after the white man's arrival, they were virtually exterminated.

These three root problems have allowed certain strongholds to become fortified in our metro area. Our city, like many other large cities, is suffering from illegal drugs, gangs, homelessness, pornography, homosexuality, prostitution, racism, violent

The Church has been called to expel evil,
demonic spirits, to tear down strongholds
and to stop sin's access into our cities.

crimes, cynical attitudes, political corruption, laws passed that highlight a self-centered, humanistic mind-set, abortion, euthanasia, legalized marijuana for medical use, worship of mother earth, New Age centers, widening rifts between the poor and the rich, teenage pregnancies, child abuse, spousal abuse, family breakdowns, a rise in the divorce rate, and AIDS. We do have a desperate situation. The city has been securely shut up behind barred gates, and the people know it not. We have given place to the devil (see Eph. 4:27). We have allowed his access into our cities, and we seem to have little concern about his occupancy. The Church has been called to expel evil, demonic spirits, to tear down strongholds and to stop sin's access into our cities.

The Greek word for place in Ephesians 4:27 is *topos*, meaning a locality, a literal home, a piece of land. *Topos* is the root word for "topographical," a geographical term. The evil we face has found a place, a home—our cities!

One of the prominent symbols of our city is a huge statue known as Portlandia. Portlandia is a huge copper statue of a woman kneeling on one knee, holding a trident in one hand while outstretching her other hand to the people on the street below. The Portland Building, on which she rests, is the seat of the government bureaucracy of our city. This statue is a source of great pride for Portland's city leaders and is a symbolic representation of the foundation and gods of our city. Portlandia's artist received his inspiration from our city seal, which contains several symbolic elements: a river, representing Portland's access to the sea via the Willamette and Columbia Rivers; a trading ship, representing the grain and other goods that go in and out of our harbor; the wagon wheel, representing the immigrants who settled Portland over the Oregon Trail; and a woman, representing Portland itself, standing on the riverbank where Portland was founded. The woman's name is Lady Commerce.

Looking at the city's symbolic representations is another way to spiritually discern its founding leaders' goals and values, godly or ungodly motives, and reasons for establishing the city. Clearly our city was established by two businessmen for the purpose of commerce, profits, money, opportunity and trade. Mammon, therefore, could have a stronghold in our city—the principality feeds off human corruption, thus corrupting our laws, our values and our spiritual endeavors.

Portlandia has a star over her head that invites the blessing of mother earth, which could be an open door to the New Age spirit and many other cults that worship nature, the sun, moon and stars. Portland worships mother earth both religiously and through land use laws, animal protection laws, and masses of environmental laws—yet abortion and euthanasia are legalized and hotly pursued in our beautiful Northwest.

FIVE DEMONIC ENTRY POINTS

Bob Beckett reveals five demonic entry points into people's lives, homes or cities:

1. **Personal Sin.** A person or city can easily open the door to demonic activity through personal sin, acts of commission or omission, works of the flesh (see Gal. 5:19-21).
2. **Generational Sin.** Committing sin is much like a physical law, such as the law of gravity, and seems to cause a spiritual genetic weakness in a family that makes its members more susceptible to that sin. The cycle, unless the blood of Christ is appropriated, can go on and on (see Exod. 20:5; Deut. 5:9).
3. **Victimization, Rejection and Trauma.** As painful and unfair as it may seem, victims of abuse, rejection and trauma are tragically vulnerable to demonization. Demons do not play fair; the younger the victim, the better. Demons serve a master who is out to steal, kill and destroy.

4. **Witchcraft, Occult and Fraternal Orders.** Conscious invitation of demonization is probable whenever deliberate involvement with or worship of gods or powers other than the true God has occurred. Few, if any, of those involved in satanic witchcraft escape demonization because they consciously open themselves up to invasion—likewise, those involved in occult aspects of the New Age movement.

5. **Cursing.** A curse is the invocation of the power of Satan or of God to negatively affect the person or thing toward which the curse is directed. The invocation may be through words or things that have been cursed or dedicated. Not every curse results in demonization, but cursing activity may open the door or encourage demonic activity.

The visible things of our daily lives—trees, people, cities, governments, professions, art forms, behavioral patterns—are commonplace and taken for granted. However, behind many visible aspects of the world around us are spiritual forces, invisible areas of reality that may have more ultimate significance than the visible (see 2 Cor. 4:18; Rom. 1:18-31,32).

Let us take courage in the following scriptures as we break into our securely shut-up cities and take back the spoils from the enemy.

Moreover the law entered that the offense might abound. But where sin abounded, grace abounded much more (Rom. 5:20).

And seek the peace of the city where I have caused you to be carried away captive, and pray to the Lord for it; for in its peace you will have peace (Jer. 29:7).

Those from among you shall build the old waste places; you shall raise up the foundations of many generations; and you shall be called the Repairer of the Breach, the Restorer of Streets to Dwell In (Isa. 58:12).

But Jesus knew their thoughts, and said to them: "Every kingdom divided against itself is brought to desolation, and every city or house divided against itself will not stand. If Satan casts out Satan, he is divided against himself. How then will his kingdom stand? And if I cast out demons by Beelzebub, by whom do your sons cast them out? Therefore they shall be your judges. But if I cast out demons by the Spirit of God, surely the kingdom of God has come upon you. Or how can one enter a strong man's house and plunder his goods, unless he first binds the strong man? And then he will plunder his house. He who is not with Me is against Me, and he who does not gather with Me scatters abroad" (Matt. 12:25-30).

Our Jericho is set before us, the Lord has spoken already, the city is already ours!

The Battle Is the Lord's
By Eugene Greco

When the battle is the Lord's,
By faith we can endure.
When the battle is the Lord's,
The victory is sure.
There is nothing to prove,
There is nothing to lose
When the battle is the Lord's.

When the battle is the Lord's,
Our faith will soon be sight.
When the battle is the Lord's,
We will not need to fight.
There is nothing to prove,
There is nothing to lose
When the battle is the Lord's;
The battle is the Lord's.

Holding onto His Word
Like a mighty sword in our hands.
With the shield of faith
And all God's armor in place,
We can stand!

In the valley of fear,
Giants drawing near, threatening.
Lord, please open our eyes,
All heaven's on our side,
We can sing!

We know the One who's in us
Is greater than he in this world.
We'll claim the ground He gives us,
Let the banners be unfurled![7]

PERSONAL APPLICATION

1. Have you reached the "entry point" to your place of promise? Your God-given promises will always be assaulted with challenges beyond your own strength, but what the enemy intends for your destruction, the

Lord will use to strengthen your faith if you will only look to Him. Where do you need to take your focus off of the obstacles and realize that the God you serve is greater than all the gods you will meet in combat?

2. Are you smart bombing your adversary through informed prayer intercession, or is your adversary smart bombing you? How much do you know about the root system of your family and your city? If you want to win the war against evil, you must first expose it. Will you begin today?

3. What are some of the symbols that represent your family or city? Are they representative of a godly root system? If not will you enter into a season of intercession to break the power of evil?

4. As you consider the five demonic entry points that Bob Beckett has revealed, can you see where Satan may have gained an access or legal right in your life or the life of your city?

Notes

1. *26 Translations of the Old Testament* (Chattanooga: AMG Publishers, 1985), p. 20.
2. Paul P. Enns, *Bible Commentary on Joshua* (Grand Rapids: Zondervan, 1981), p. 57.
3. Arnold Toynbee, *Cities of Destiny* (New York: McGraw-Hill, 1967), n. p.
4. Bob Beckett, *Committment to Conquer* (Grand Rapids: Chosen Books, 1997), p. 79.
5. George Otis, Jr., *Informed Intercession* (Ventura, CA: Regal Books, 1999), prepublication manuscript.
6. Harold Caballeros, *The Transforming Power of Revival* (Buenos Aires, Argentina: Peniel, 1998), pp. 15, 16.
7. Eugene Greco, "The Battle Is the Lord's," His Banner Publishing, 1997. Used with permission.

KEYS TO THE
CITY AND
THE CITY
CHURCH

And the Lord said to Joshua: "See! I have given Jericho into your hand."

JOSHUA 6:2

The misplacement of my keys is an ongoing saga at the Damazio house. My wife of 23 years does not panic when she hears my frustrated self-murmuring, "What did I do with those keys? I am sure someone has taken them—one of the children, no doubt!"

She offers a few comments, usually something such as, "Well, this is certainly the first time Dad has lost his keys! What must we do to solve this mystery? Where will they be found?" And then, the worst happens: She heads directly for the spot where the keys have been misplaced. How humiliating! But, without the keys, the car doesn't go, the office doesn't open, and private entryways become forbidden entryways.

THE KEYS TO THE CITY

As Joshua faced Jericho, he needed the keys for the entryway into the city. He did not know the names of the keys, nor could he find the key to Jericho without the locksmith—in this case, the angel of the Lord.

Every city has entry points, doors that are locked securely by the underworld's invisible forces. We need a locksmith. We need the master key. Jesus said in Matthew 16:19: "I will give you the keys of the kingdom of heaven, and whatever you bind on earth will be bound in heaven, and whatever you loose on earth will be loosed in heaven."

The keys have been given to the Church. This statement may sound very elementary, but it is, in fact, foundational to all city-reaching activity. The Church is the vehicle God has chosen to use as His keys for unlocking the doors and gates of the cities. Keys are to be used in shutting or opening that which is locked. The Keeper of the Keys has the power to open and to shut; this power denotes God-given authority, authority that has been given to the Church.

The city has been given into the hands of the Church in the city—not to one particular church, but to the whole Church in the city. When we speak of city reaching, it is always in the context of a unified majority of the Church in a city working together to reach the entire city. Thus, the enemy works hard to keep the Church in the city divided, fragmented, isolated and polarized. Fears, intimidation, competitive attitudes, insecurities and carnalities are used by demonic forces to ensure that the Church does not find the keys to the city. But Scripture tells us that Jesus desires to give us the key of David that opens shut cities:

> "And to the angel of the church in Philadelphia write,
> 'These things says He who is holy, He who is true, He

who has the key of David, He who opens and no one shuts, and shuts and no one opens: I know your works. See, I have set before you an open door, and no one can shut it; for you have a little strength, have kept My word, and have not denied My name'" (Rev. 3:7,8).

GOD GIVES THE RIGHT KEY AND THE RIGHT APPROACH

Our cities have been securely shut up, locked, bolted and declared off-limits by our enemy. But Jericho was not impregnable, and Jericho was not built to withstand the army that possessed the right key and the right approach. The key may seem insulting to human reasoning; it may even be mocked by human intellect, or for that matter, rejected by a carnal program-driven church that can't see anything outside its own programs. However, the keys will be given to the humble, the intercessors of the city, the servant-driven churches.

The religious community is sometimes like the Pharisees of old who took away the key of knowledge (see Luke 11:52), not going in themselves and even hindering those who might try to enter in. Our cities have already been given to us by the work of Christ on the cross and promises in God's Word. We have a great and effective door ready to open for us in our cities:

For a great and effective door has opened to me, and there are many adversaries (1 Cor. 16:9).

The following are some biblical observations concerning cities:

• Each city has its own unique city personality and city destiny (see Rev. 1–3).

- Each city has its own cry that ascends to heaven—God hears that cry (see Gen. 18:21; Isa. 14:3).
- God measures, limits and judges the integrity of each city (see Matt. 11:20-24; 23:35-38).
- God uses various means to speak clearly to each city (see Prov. 1:20,21; 8:1-7; Micah 6:9).
- God prepares, anoints and sends specific ministries to specific cities (see Jonah 1:2; Luke 9:51-56).
- God has a master key for each individual city (see John 4; Acts 14:27; 2 Cor. 2:12).
- God sets the Church to stand in the gap and intercede for the city (see Gen. 18,19; Ezek. 9:1-7; 22:30,37).
- God deals with the Church about how it relates to the city (see Rev. 1—3).
- God holds the elders of the city responsible for its spiritual state (see Deut. 19:11,12; 21:1-9; Ezek. 3:17-21; 33:1-9).
- God weeps over the city's spiritual destiny (see Luke 19:41).

The previous observations are very clear concerning God's burden for and involvement with the cities of our world. The keys are available, but only to the Church in the city, the true Church as described in Matthew 16:16-18:

Simon Peter answered and said, "You are the Christ, the Son of the living God." Jesus answered and said to him, "Blessed are you, Simon Bar-Jonah, for flesh and blood has not revealed this to you, but My Father who is in heaven. And I also say to you that you are Peter, and on this rock I will build My church, and the gates of Hades shall not prevail against it."

ONE CHURCH, MANY CONGREGATIONS

The Church in the city refers to the whole Church, no matter what denominational or nondenominational title it may hold. All congregations that are biblically consistent with the New Testament definition of the Church make up the Church in the city. Not national or international, denominational or nondenominational, sectarian or nonsectarian—the Church is one new man, one Body and one people.

Bob Beckett says, "But this brings us to a major weakness Satan has taken advantage of since the days of Paul and Apollos: disunity among believers. Paul vented a bit of exasperation at the young Corinthian church for being divided over its preference of religious leaders in 1 Corinthians 1:10: 'Now I plead with you, brethren, by the name of our Lord Jesus Christ, that you all speak the same thing, and that there be no divisions among you.' How much farther along are we who live on the brink of the twenty-first century than believers in first-century Corinth? If we judge our progress by the unity demonstrated today in the Body of Christ, it would seem that we have not gained much understanding in the past two thousand years!"[1]

The Church Jesus speaks of in Matthew 16:16-18 is the Church universal—the Church used in terms of God's general and overall plan for the whole of humanity and the universe. In Matthew 16:16-18, Jesus speaks of the local congregation as His Church. The church, when used in relation to a local body of believers, speaks to us of actual people who form a concrete expression of the manifestation of the universal Church. One is abstract, the other is concrete; one is mystical, the other is tangible; one is universal, the other is local.

The City Church is made up of many Christ-led congregations or local churches. This is a biblical model and one that is easily followed in the New Testament. Every local church must have its own eldership, personality and focus, but in all that we do, we should seek to glorify God and work together as one Church. Local churches are addressed in the New Testament:

> Simon Peter answered and said, "You are the Christ, the Son of the living God." Jesus answered and said to him, "Blessed are you, Simon Bar-Jonah, for flesh and blood has not revealed this to you, but My Father who is in heaven. And I also say to you that you are Peter, and on this rock I will build My church, and the gates of Hades shall not prevail against it" (Matt. 16:16-18).

> So when they had appointed elders in every church, and prayed with fasting, they commended them to the Lord in whom they had believed (Acts 14:23).

> Likewise greet the church that is in their house. Greet my beloved Epaenetus, who is the firstfruits of Achaia to Christ (Rom. 16:5).

> For you indeed give thanks well, but the other is not edified (1 Cor. 14:17).

> Or to governors, as to those who are sent by him for the punishment of evildoers and for the praise of those who do good (1 Pet. 2:14).

THE CHURCH DEFINED

The Greek word *ekklesia* translated "church" in our English Bible simply means "those who are called out." The term was used to designate the gathering or assembling of the citizens of a city who were called out by the herald for the transaction of public business. We, as local congregations in the city, make up a City Church that is called out of darkness and called out of our own programs to accomplish a Kingdom purpose.

Baker's Dictionary of Theology defines the "Church" clearly:

The New Testament word *ekklesia* is used of a public assemblage summoned by a herald (see Acts 19:32,39,41). In the LXX, however, it means the assembly or congregation of the Israelites, especially when gathered before the Lord for religious purposes. Accordingly, it is used in the New Testament for the congregation that the living God assembles about His Messiah Jesus. Thus the Church is the spiritual family of God, the Christian fellowship created by the Holy Spirit through the testimony to the mighty acts of God in Christ Jesus. More fully stated, the one Church of God is not an institutional but a supernatural entity that is in the process of growth toward the world to come. All its members are in Christ and knit together by a supernatural kinship. All their gifts and activities continue the work of Christ by the power of the Holy Spirit, originate from Christ, and are coordinated by Him to the final goal.[2]

The following verses help to define the goal of the Church:

I have set watchmen on your walls, O Jerusalem; they shall never hold their peace day or night. You who make mention of the LORD, do not keep silent, and give Him no rest till He establishes and till He makes Jerusalem a praise in the earth (Isa. 62:6,7).

Now it came to pass at the end of seven days that the word of the LORD came to me, saying, "Son of man, I have made you a watchman for the house of Israel; therefore hear a word from My mouth, and give them warning from Me: When I say to the wicked, 'You shall surely die,' and you give him no warning, nor speak to warn the wicked from his wicked way, to save his life, that same wicked man shall die in his iniquity; but his blood I will require at your hand. Yet, if you warn the wicked, and he does not turn from his wickedness, nor from his wicked way, he shall die in his iniquity; but you have delivered your soul" (Ezek. 3:16-19).

Many Pastors, One City Church

The eldership of the city is made up of overseeing leaders from all the congregations; these leaders become the watchmen on the wall for their particular local churches. One individual pastor cannot pastor the whole city, but together all the city pastors are called to pastor all the city. The City Church becomes responsible for those in the fold and for those outside the fold, the whole city becomes the Church's parish, the whole city becomes the Church's vineyard (see Jer. 12:10; 23:3,4). Note how the churches were addressed in the New Testament:

CHURCHES ADDRESSED IN A REGION
- Churches in Galilee (Acts 9:31)
- Churches in Judea (Acts 9:31)
- Churches in Samaria (Acts 9:31)
- Churches in Cilicia (Acts 15:41)
- Churches in Syria (Acts 15:41)
- Churches in Asia (1 Cor. 16:19; Rev. 1:4)
- Churches in Galatia (Gal. 1:2)

CHURCHES ADDRESSED IN A CITY

- Church in Corinth (1 Cor. 1:2; 2 Cor. 1:1)
- Church in Thessalonica (1 Thess. 1:1; 2 Thess. 1:1)
- Church in Ephesus (Rev. 1:11; 2:1)
- Church in Smyrna (Rev. 1:11; 2:8)
- Church in Pergamos (Rev. 1:11; 2:12)
- Church in Thyatira (Rev. 1:11; 2:18)
- Church in Sardis (Rev. 1:11; 3:1)
- Church in Philadelphia (Rev. 1:11; 3:7)
- Church in Laodicea (Rev. 1:11; 3:14)
- Church in Jerusalem (Acts 8:1; 11:22)
- Church in Antioch (Acts 13:1)

We recognize that scripturally there are local congregations that have locally appointed eldership and ministries, Body life and God-given purposes for existence. These local congregations work together in a given locality as the expression of the Body of Christ in each city—what we are calling the "City Church."

One Church, Many Identities

A proper perspective of local congregations helps us to have a proper perspective on the City Church. The keys for the city will be given to the watchmen on the wall representing the whole Church in the city—not one watchman, but one united leadership. Scripture predicts that the Church will be unified (see Isa. 52:8; Jer. 3:18). Jesus Himself prayed that the Church would have the same union with one another as He had with the Father (see John 17:11,21-23). Jesus taught that there is one fold and one Shepherd (see John 10:16) and that the city elders are His under-shepherds (see Jer. 3:15, 23:4; Acts 20:28; 1 Pet. 5:2). Each local congregation has at least four particular identifiable marks:

1. EACH CHURCH HAS ITS OWN DIVINE DESTINY

The divine destiny is facilitated by the type of overseeing leadership the Lord places over each local congregation. This book's purpose, however, is not to discuss church leadership, church government and church function, which is a broad subject and one with varying degrees of application. Our belief is that a church is led by a "set man" with a team of elders who work with the set man to fulfill vision.

In my book *Effective Keys to Successful Leadership,* I define the set man as, "A helmsman who stands in his leadership position to direct and manage the Church in all areas of spiritual life and vision. He steers the ship according to his God-given gift to lead, his biblical knowledge of the God-given vision and his proven character. He has the ability to raise up leaders and work in a teamlike manner in order to equip the church for its God-given task."[3]

As God anoints and directs the set man with a powerful vision or dream, it will energize everyone around him. The gift-mix of the overseeing pastor will have great influence upon the vision of that particular church. The church may take on an apostolic, evangelistic, pastoral, teaching or prophetic spiritual chemistry according to the gift-mix of the set leader.

In every city these different types of churches can be discerned. We may describe a church as an Antioch church because of its apostolic church-planting nature, a Jerusalem church because of its teaching focus, a Corinthian church because of its focus on the gifts of the Spirit, or an Ephesus church because of its regional influence, apostolic doctrine and world focus.

2. EACH LOCAL CHURCH HAS ITS OWN UNIQUE PERSONALITY

Personality describes the unique methods, procedures, philosophy and style of the local church. Personality is not the doctrinal or concrete biblical essence of the church; it is the freedom found within that church to apply and pursue truth through its own unique personality. No two families do everything the same. They may both celebrate birthdays, holidays and special family occasions, but how they celebrate is very different. To promote unity and to assure variety at the same time, we must give room for church personality within our City Church. We all love God and worship God, but this is done not according to hard-core biblical guidelines only but also according to church personality.

We must be on guard not to judge others' personalities as nonbiblical because they don't fit ours.

Hymns or choruses, fast or slow, contemporary or traditional, short or long sermons, prayer offered silently or with plenty of joyful noises—the Bible allows for a variety of expressions. We must be on guard not to judge others' personalities as nonbiblical because they doesn't fit ours. Let us not meddle in other church's affairs, because in reality things are often very different than they appear from our perspective. The Scripture compares intruding in other people's affairs to grabbing an angry dog by his ears (see Prov. 26:17); you will be bitten whether you hang on or let go. We should not tease or make jokes about other churches' personalities any more than we should do this to another individual. Teasing not only provokes strife between churches and church leaderships, but can also cause irreparable damage and hurt (see Prov. 26:18,19).

3. EACH LOCAL CHURCH HAS ITS OWN DOMINANT BIBLICAL DISTINCTIVES

Distinctives are usually a practical outworking of the church leadership's vision and mission established over a long period of time. Distinctives and vision values are nurtured by continual feeding upon the Word of God by the leadership team. These distinctives vary from church to church and, again, can be a source of discord and doubt among City Churches.

If one church has dominant distinctives in the area of preaching salvation resulting in an evangelistic focus, an evangelistic atmosphere and an evangelistic congregation, the teaching-dominant church might unwisely criticize, judge or simply drop disparaging slams against this church such as, "Shallow. Not enough doctrine. Imbalanced. Not going to last." All of these judgments could be removed if church leadership and church laypeople would only make room for churches with dominant distinctive differences from their own.

Evangelistic, family focused, worship centered, teaching based, missions minded, city-prayer concentrated, social-causes oriented, leadership-training focused—all of these distinctives are rarely found in one church. We all have our focus points. If local churches would minister to the city as one Church, one Body, we would probably have all the distinctives needed in our corporate City Church to supernaturally impact the city.

4. EACH LOCAL CHURCH HAS A RESPONSIBILITY TO FULFILL A UNIQUE GOD-GIVEN VISION AND MISSION

The vision of a local church is a reflection of its doctrinal and biblical distinctives, its own specific church history and its present leadership. Each local church vision will be different—not wrong or sub-Bible because it's not like the church you go to, just different. Chuck Swindoll offers some sound advice on answering the question, Why are we in existence as a local church?

> The array of possible answers might be: to present the gospel to the lost, to bring hope to the hurting, to provide a place of worship and instruction, to equip saints for the work of the ministry, to comfort the grieving, to feed the hungry, to help the needy. While all of these are certainly worthwhile reasons and part of the greater picture, they are not the primary reasons for the Church's existence. The answer is "to glorify the Lord our God."[4]

The following Scriptures clarify our purpose as a Church, which is to glorify the Lord:

> Therefore, whether you eat or drink, or whatever you do, do all to the glory of God (1 Cor. 10:31).

> Therefore we also pray always for you that our God would count you worthy of this calling, and fulfill all the good pleasure of His goodness and the work of faith with power (2 Thess. 1:11).

> Let your light so shine before men, that they may see your good works and glorify your Father in heaven (Matt. 5:16).

Clearly all churches have this basic mandate: to glorify God. This is our mission statement, our purpose and our vision. The taproot purpose of our existence is just what the *Westminster*

Shorter Catechism suggests: to glorify God and to enjoy Him forever. How each local church glorifies God will be unique and with a broad scope of application. The attitude of the local church leadership will be reflected in the local church congregation.

Our responsibility is to glorify God in all that we do and to encourage and to lift up all other churches in our cities that are seeking to do the same. Undoubtedly we should desire to be as blessed and as big as God will allow us to become and to achieve as much as He will permit. Scripture clearly shows that whatever part of God's purpose we fail to complete will be a matter for personal judgment at the judgment seat of Christ (see 1 Cor. 3:10-15).

Conversely, we should be satisfied to be or to do as little as God is content to allow. There is no virtue in trying to do more than God has commanded or in struggling to be more than He has made us to be. It is enough for each church to simply fulfill the Father's plan, whether that confines us to comparative obscurity or carries us to astonishing renown (see Prov. 23:4,5; 25:27; Eccles. 4:6). Our vision must first be deeply rooted in bringing glory to God, focused upon Christ and His work, and carried out by obedience.

God has a key for the City Church to unlock every city. The book of Acts reveals examples of cities impacted by ministries with the right key at the right time with the right attitude.

City	Scripture	Keys to Cities
Sychar	John 4:28-30, 39-42	One covert, personal miracle, one woman
Jerusalem	Acts 1–4	Prayer, supernatural outpouring
Samaria	Acts 8	Philip the Evangelist
Joppa	Acts 9:36-42	Healing of Dorcas, dead raised

City	Scripture	Keys to Cities
Caesarea	Acts 10	House meeting, outpouring of the Holy Spirit
Antioch	Acts 11	Common men preaching, lay ministries
Lystra	Acts 14	Miracle of the lame man
Philippi	Acts 16	House meeting, miracle earthquake
Thessalonica	Acts 17	Teaching
Corinth	Acts 18	Demonstration of the Holy Spirit

Like Joshua, we face our securely shut up cities, but not without divine directions from the Captain of the Lord of Hosts. In the Old Testament, the people of God faced many walled cities with a warrior king and armies residing inside. In the natural, there was no way to penetrate these impregnable cities except by divine revelation, the God key (see Num. 13:28; Deut. 1:28; Josh. 6:5,20; Heb. 11:30). We are world turners, keys—we turn cities right side up!

PERSONAL APPLICATION

1. Do you have a "City Church" mind-set, or are you in competition with and isolated from the other churches in your city? If you are not connected with other churches, are you willing to be used as God's key for unlocking the disunity in your city?
2. Have you grabbed an angry dog by his ears lately? In other words, have you been critical of other churches that do not "do church" the way you do? Have you spread spiritual rabies by backbiting those who are different from you?

3. Whatever part of God's purpose we fail to complete will be a matter for personal judgment. What is your purpose? If you cannot define your purpose, will you spend some time in prayer with fasting to gain a vision of the purpose for your life, your church and your city? Write out your purpose statement and keep it before you at all times.

4. Whose leadership role is being glorified by your life—God's or your own? Have you been fulfilling your own need to be recognized, or are you content to glorify God at any cost?

Notes

1. Bob Beckett, *Commitment to Conquer* (Grand Rapids: Chosen Books, 1997), pp. 116, 117.
2. Everett F. Harrison, Editor, *Baker's Dictionary of Theology* (Grand Rapids: Baker Book House, 1960), p. 123.
3. Frank Damazio, *Effective Keys to Successful Leadership* (Portland, OR: Bible Press, 1993), p. 15.
4. Chuck Swindoll, *The Church Purpose, Profile and Priorities* (Fullerton, CA: Insight for Living, 1987), p. 2.

CHAPTER 9

TRANSFORMING
CHURCHES TO
REACH CITIES

"I will build My church, and the gates of Hades shall not prevail against it. And I will give you the keys of the kingdom of heaven, and whatever you bind on earth will be bound in heaven, and whatever you loose on earth will be loosed in heaven."

MATTHEW 16:18,19

In A.D. 374 Saint Jerome, scolding a monk for having abandoned the desert for the city, wrote, "O wasteland bright with the spring flowers of Christ! O solitude out of which come these stones that build the city of the great King in the Apocalypse! O desolate desert rejoicing in God's familiar presence! What keeps you in the world, O brother? You are above and beyond the world. How long is the shade of the house going to conceal you? How long shall the grimy prisons of those cities intern you?"[1]

REASONS FOR THE ANTI-CITY ATTITUDE

Jerome had an anti-city attitude: He could not reconcile how the Church could have any relationship to the city. Jerome was probably reacting to the ancient Greek city-state belief that the city was a religious community. Its citizens were those who would trace their roots back to the god or gods responsible for the city. Citizenship carried the right and obligation to worship the city's many gods at the civic shrines. To be ostracized was to be forbidden to enter the city walls. To live outside the city walls was to live outside the god's blessings.

The terms "pagan" and "heathen" originally denoted those who lived outside the city walls, outside of the god's blessings. Jerome, along with many other monks and spiritual leaders, withdrew his life and ministry outside the city. How could the Church be in the city but not of it? How would the Church function as an alien citizen?

Tertullian, another Church father, had a Christ-against-the-city posture. Tertullian's Christian life was an urgent attempt to escape the pollution and idolatrous decay of the urban life surrounding the Christian.

Augustine promoted another view in his book *The City of God*, proclaiming a new model for understanding the Christian view of the city. Augustine's view was Christ the Transformer of the City, or Christ for the City.

A SICK CHURCH CANNOT HEAL A SICK CITY

Christ redirects, reinvigorates and regenerates the life within the city through the Church. Jesus comes to the city in disorder to heal and renew what sin has infected—to restore and to redirect what has been perverted. The culture of the city is not discarded by this work of regeneration; it is redirected by the power of the Kingdom. These two opposite viewpoints are also present in the Church of the twenty-first century. My desire is to see Christ as the Transformer of Cities and to see the Church as the power force behind this work of transformation.

A sick Church cannot heal a sick city.

A dead Church cannot bring life to a dead city.

A divided Church cannot bring peace and

unity to a divided city.

If the Church is to become the city-reaching vessel it is called to be, the Church itself must be transformed before it can be a transformer. A sick Church cannot heal a sick city. A dead Church cannot bring life to a dead city. A divided Church cannot bring peace and unity to a divided city. A weak Church does not have the spiritual power to bring about change. The Church in the city desperately needs a spiritual transformation, a new soul, a new heart, a new spirit. I believe the keys to the city are given to the Church in the city, making the health of the Church of prime importance.

I've heard of many city-reaching plans in the making, some already being implemented, that make little mention of the importance of healthy local pastors and local churches. But how will city reaching occur if God's chosen instrument is not prepared to reach the people in the city by becoming spiritually discerning and able to confront evil powers, equipped to pray, willing to worship God and know God's Word, and ready to love and assimilate new people? This is a huge problem that must be overcome if we are to see our cities impacted with spiritual fruit that remains.

We must learn how to engage in spiritual warfare, do prayer-walking, minister to the poor, meet the social needs in our cities, and transform our churches into places where the spiritual atmosphere is charged with the authentic power and presence of Christ. The Church must create an atmosphere in which the love of God is evident in relationships, reaching out to the new convert, the new single, the new alternative-lifestyle person. If we do not learn these things, the Church will not be able to assimilate the harvest of souls jolted free from darkness through city-reaching activity.

The Church is not only to be concerned with city reaching; it should also be concerned with city keeping. The longevity of city ministry is certainly tied to the spiritual health of the churches in the city. The goal of city evangelism is city disciple making, which necessitates spiritually healthy and motivated people.

LIFE-THREATENING DISEASES THAT INFECT THE CHURCH

In his book *The Healthy Church*, Peter Wagner lists nine diseases that threaten the health of all local churches:[2]

1. **Ethnikitis.** Because Ethnikitis is caused by contextual factors, it is probably more helpful to focus attention on the changing community rather than the changing

church. The problem usually revolves around a static church in a changing neighborhood.

2. **Ghost Town Disease.** The underlying cause of Ghost Town Disease is a deteriorating community; people are moving out, but no one is moving in. A church dies of natural causes which is not necessarily tragic.

3. **People Blindness.** Most churches are not aware of this disease; they are in active denial that they could possibly have it. People Blindness is the malady that prevents us from seeing the important cultural differences that exist between groups of people living in geographical proximity to one another, differences that tend to create barriers to the acceptance of our message.

4. **Hyper-Cooperativism.** This occurs when an attempt is made to use cooperation for unwise purposes. It is frequently not just neutral; in certain circumstances it can become counterproductive.

5. **Koinonitis.** *Koinonia,* the Greek word for fellowship, is a healthy and vital part of a growing church. When *koinonia* becomes Koinonitis, interpersonal relationships tend to become so deep and so mutually absorbing that they can be regarded as the central focal point for almost all church activity and involvement. When this is allowed to occur, church programs tend to become centripetal, drawing participants inward toward each other, rather than centrifugal, pushing people outward to reach others for Christ.

6. **Sociological Strangulation.** This disease is found in growing churches, not plateaued or declining churches. It is a slowdown in the rate of church growth caused when the flow of people into the church begins to exceed the capacity of the facilities to accommodate it.

In other words, a church, like a plant, can become pot-bound if the root system becomes too big for the pot.

7. **Arrested Spiritual Development.** When people in the church are not growing in the things of God or in their relationships with one another, the total health of the church deteriorates and the church cannot grow. This disease is connected with internal growth, sometimes referred to as quality growth. This disease is prominent in the American church: churches barely limping along, implementing a program, raising a budget, hiring a preacher, conducting worship services, and doing whatever else churches are supposed to do, but merely going through the motions.

8. **Saint John's Syndrome.** This disease is simply when Christians become Christians in name only. When faith is only routine, when church involvement is largely going through the motions, and when belonging to church is nothing more than a family tradition and a social nicety, Saint John's Syndrome is likely at work.

9. **Hypopneumia.** Is defined as subnormal ministry of the Holy Spirit in a Christian individual, a church or a Christian group. From the Greek words *hypo*, meaning below, and *pneuma*, meaning wind or spirit. Hypopneumia is rooted in spiritual factors.

You may want to give your church or ministry a spiritual physical—a check-up, an evaluation to ensure that your ministry is symptom free of these nine diseases. With the Holy Spirit's help, we can transform our churches into healthy city-reaching and city-keeping churches.

As spiritual leaders, pastors, elders, missionaries and church planters, we must seek to build "New Testament quality" churches.

New Testament churches are local churches founded upon the patterns and principles of the divine order given in the New Testament for what the Church is to be. The New Testament church (1) comes together to fulfill God's purposes, (2) is structured to a New Testament pattern, and (3) is expanding and impacting its neighborhoods, city and region with the gospel. A New Testament church profile can be seen in the first seven chapters of Acts.

FIFTEEN MARKS OF A NEW TESTAMENT CHURCH

Chapters 1–7 of Acts describe the first seven years of the Church Christ built after His ascension. These chapters describe the "kingdom of God" culture in terms of priorities and practices. As we become churches that can spiritually impact our cities, these discernible marks of a New Testament church are vitally important. The following are 15 essential marks of a city-reaching church as found in these seven chapters:

1. A SPIRITUALLY POWERFUL CHURCH

   But you shall receive power when the Holy Spirit has come upon you; and you shall be witnesses to Me in Jerusalem, and in all Judea and Samaria, and to the end of the earth (Acts 1:8).

2. AN AGGRESSIVELY WITNESSING CHURCH

   But you shall receive power when the Holy Spirit has come upon you; and you shall be witnesses to Me in Jerusalem, and in all Judea and Samaria, and to the end of the earth (Acts 1:8).

3. A CHURCH COMMITTED TO CONTINUAL PRAYER

   These all continued with one accord in prayer and supplication, with the women and Mary the mother of Jesus, and with His brothers (Acts 1:14).

4. A UNIFIED CHURCH

When the Day of Pentecost had fully come, they were all with one accord in one place (Acts 2:1).

5. A SPIRIT-FILLED CHURCH

When the Day of Pentecost had fully come, they were all with one accord in one place. And suddenly there came a sound from heaven, as of a rushing mighty wind, and it filled the whole house where they were sitting. Then there appeared to them divided tongues, as of fire, and one sat upon each of them. And they were all filled with the Holy Spirit and began to speak with other tongues, as the Spirit gave them utterance (Acts 2:1-4).

Then Peter said to them, "Repent, and let every one of you be baptized in the name of Jesus Christ for the remission of sins; and you shall receive the gift of the Holy Spirit" (Acts 2:38).

6. A WORD-CENTERED CHURCH

And they continued steadfastly in the apostles' doctrine and fellowship, in the breaking of bread, and in prayers (Acts 2:42).

7. A GOD-HEARING CHURCH

Then fear came upon every soul, and many wonders and signs were done through the apostles (Acts 2:43).

8. A SHARING CHURCH

So continuing daily with one accord in the temple, and breaking bread from house to house, they ate their food with gladness and simplicity of heart (Acts 2:46).

9. A GATHERING-TOGETHER CHURCH

So continuing daily with one accord in the temple, and breaking bread from house to house, they ate their food with gladness and simplicity of heart (Acts 2:46).

10. A SUPERNATURAL-BELIEVING CHURCH

And suddenly there came a sound from heaven, as of a rushing mighty wind, and it filled the whole house where they were sitting (Acts 2:2).

Now God worked unusual miracles by the hands of Paul, so that even handkerchiefs or aprons were brought from his body to the sick, and the diseases left them and the evil spirits went out of them (Acts 19:11,12).

11. A FELLOWSHIPPING, RELATING CHURCH

So continuing daily with one accord in the temple, and breaking bread from house to house, they ate their food with gladness and simplicity of heart (Acts 2:46).

12. A REJOICING CHURCH

So continuing daily with one accord in the temple, and breaking bread from house to house, they ate their food with gladness and simplicity of heart (Acts 2:46).

13. A WORSHIPING CHURCH

So continuing daily with one accord in the temple, and breaking bread from house to house, they ate their food with gladness and simplicity of heart (Acts 2:46).

"And with this the words of the prophets agree, just as it is written: 'After this I will return and will rebuild the tabernacle of David, which has fallen down; I will rebuild its ruins, and I will set it up; so that the rest of mankind may seek the LORD, even all the Gentiles who are called by My name, says the LORD who does all these things'" (Acts 15:15-17).

14. A PEOPLE-DRAWING CHURCH

Praising God and having favor with all the people. And the Lord added to the church daily those who were being saved (Acts 2:47).

15. A GROWING, EXPANDING CHURCH

Praising God and having favor with all the people. And the Lord added to the church daily those who were being saved (Acts 2:47).

These are only the marks from the first seven chapters of Acts; obviously, we could add many more from the rest of Acts and the Epistles. Other marks would include an apostolic church, prophetic church, global-missions church and more. These 15 are basic enough for all leaders to put a hand on and build into their churches.

THE HEARTBEAT OF A HEALTHY CHURCH

The Jerusalem church did impact its city and the cities in the Roman Empire. But very quickly the Jerusalem church's numerical expansion threatened to undo its blessed success. The Jerusalem church became a metachurch, signifying both a change of mind about how ministry is to be done and a change of form in the church's infrastructure. To build churches that grow, we must understand the needed heartbeat of the church.

The balanced heartbeat of a healthy city-reaching church is what I call the corporate and the cell. Let me illustrate this in a simple diagram as taken from the Scriptures in chapters 2, 4 and 5 of Acts:

THE CORPORATE

GATHERING OF THE WHOLE CHURCH

- **CELEBRATION**
- **PREACHING**
- **DIRECTION**
- **EQUIPPING**
- **EDIFICATION**

ACTS 1:14; 2:1,41,44;
HEB. 10:24,25;
2 CHRON. 5:11-14

THE CELL

CHURCH MEETING IN SMALL GROUPS

- **INFILTRATION**
- **SHARING**
- **DISCIPLING**
- **ENCOURAGING**
- **EXPANDING**

ACTS 20:20; ROM. 14:7;
HEB. 3:13; MATT. 28:19,20;
1JOHN 3:14-18; COL. 1:28,29

In preparing our church for ministering to and penetrating the city with the gospel, we have developed both the power of the corporate and the net ministry of the cell, our small groups. The identifying, equipping and releasing of lay ministry is a key to building a city-reaching church (see Acts 6:1-7). We have added to our ministry team lay pastors along with staff pastors. The lay pastors are equipped to do all aspects of ministry. They oversee our cells, as this is our strategy for reaching every neighborhood in our city.

Our cells are being developed to implement our city-reaching strategies. The corporate, or the public gathering, is absolutely necessary and has a defined purpose, but without the cells, the church will not become a New Testament church that meets both in the temple and house to house.

A church that bottlenecks its outreach by depending on its specialists, its paid staff, to do the ministry is living in violation of both the intentions of its head, Christ, and the consistent pattern of the Early Church as seen in Acts 1—7. We must have a biblical heartbeat. Both the corporate and cell are needed if we are to be city-reaching churches.

DEVELOPING DYNAMIC CORPORATE GATHERINGS

Scripture is very clear in establishing the importance of corporate gatherings:

> In the name of our Lord Jesus Christ, when you are gathered together, along with my spirit, with the power of our Lord Jesus Christ (1 Cor. 5:4).

> Therefore when you come together in one place, it is not to eat the Lord's Supper (1 Cor. 11:20).

> Therefore, my brethren, when you come together to eat, wait for one another (1 Cor. 11:33).

Therefore if the whole church comes together in one place, and all speak with tongues, and there come in those who are uninformed or unbelievers, will they not say that you are out of your mind? (1 Cor. 14:23).

How is it then, brethren? Whenever you come together, each of you has a psalm, has a teaching, has a tongue, has a revelation, has an interpretation. Let all things be done for edification (1 Cor. 14:26).

- Are we satisfied with the spiritual quality of our public gatherings?
- Are we accomplishing our short-range and long-range benefits for the people?
- Are we diluting our corporate gatherings with things that do not edify the flock or help the service?
- Are we approaching our corporate gatherings with prayerfulness, as well as defined goals and purposes?
- Are we following any traditions or procedures that have little or no biblical base and in fact are hindering a fresh flow of the Holy Spirit?
- Are we in a spiritual rut that is causing stagnation and spiritual death?

Corporate gathering times are meant to impart spiritual health and strength to our congregations. The Hebrew definitions of the word "assemble" are particularly descriptive of what corporate gatherings should be. This word "assemble" denotes to grasp, to collect together, to scrape together, to go forth and assemble as a man of war, to assemble against the enemy, a convocation together for a sacred thing, a gathering together in one place, to meet with someone at an appointed time, to come together for a

specific purpose at a specific time and place. (See Exod. 33:8;
Lev. 8:4; 23:36; Num. 1:18; 8:9; 10:2,3; 20:6-8; Josh. 18:1; 1 Sam. 2:22;
2 Sam. 20:4,5; 2 Chron. 5:6; Ps. 89:7; 107:32; 111:1; Prov. 5:14;
Isa. 4:5; 43:9; 45:20; Joel 2:6; 3:1; Acts 1:4; 4:31; 11:26; 15:25.)

The best known New Testament scripture for the corporate
gathering is found in Hebrews 10:24,25:

> And let us consider one another in order to stir up love
> and good works, not forsaking the assembling of our-
> selves together, as is the manner of some, but exhorting
> one another, and so much the more as you see the Day
> approaching.

The implication here is that those who neglect corporate
gatherings eventually become isolated from the Spirit's movement in the local church. After a prolonged period of neglect,
the believer can become spiritually deprived.

God commanded Israel to appear before Him consistently
and often. The idea of "appearing before the Lord" is to be
inspected, to expose oneself to scrutiny. Its meaning can be seen
in the act of flaying and inspecting a sacrificial animal that
would reveal its inward parts. God commanded Israel to appear
before Him to accomplish five purposes:

1. Personal inspection (see Ps. 139:23).
2. Spiritual renewal (see Isa. 57:14,15).
3. Rehearsing the Word (see Neh. 8:1-12).
4. Renewing our vows (see Ps. 61).
5. Spiritual enlargement (see Exod. 34:24; Ps. 119:32).

The city in which you have been placed is in need of the
supernatural presence and power of God. Since the church

meets corporately more than 150 times a year, can your city find in these meetings power, presence, healing, anointed words, forgiveness, gifts of the Spirit, life-changing worship, life itself?

In the apostle Paul's teaching on the corporate gathering of a church found in 1 Corinthians 14, he gives seven vital functions of corporate meetings: edification, exhortation, comfort, revelation, knowledge, prophecy and doctrine. As we practice these vital principles in our corporate gatherings, a dynamic explosion of God's presence can consistently happen. Corporate gatherings are a major source of spiritual strength for families, singles, youth, business people and those from our city who have never been exposed to God's life-changing presence.

DEVELOPING SMALL GROUP MINISTRY CALLED THE "CELL"

The balanced heartbeat of the city-reaching church is a spiritually powerful corporate public gathering and a spiritually healthy small-group ministry. Churches must recognize the need for developing a structure that will incorporate opportunities for building and nurturing relationships—relationships with other believers and relationships with unbelievers.

The city cell ministry of our church is a vital part of our strategy in reaching our city. Houses, or home-based ministries, may be the most perfectly suited means for reaching the post-Christian generation with the gospel. The home of every believer connected to a healthy life-giving local church will become a life-giving home. These homes can become centers of spiritual activity, places where divine surgery can take place in people's lives. The cell is a group of people who have made a commitment to relate to one another with increasing depth, authenticity, honesty and vulnerability. I created an acronym for cells that defines our church's purpose, mission and function:

Connecting people relationally.
Encouraging and equipping every believer to be a disciple of Christ.
Learning to use our homes as ministry centers.
Loosing people from the powers of darkness.
Strategic creative ministry to impact our immediate geographical area.

As the Church has a balanced heartbeat, so does the cell ministry. The heartbeat of the cell is:

City-Cell Life which describes the shepherding, pastoral ministry aspect of the cell, caring for and ministering to every person through the cell seven days a week. This is the spirit of community seen in Acts 2:42-47—the *koinonia* spirit of partnership, sharing, relationship, intimacy, accountability, support and extended family.

City-Cell Reach which describes the evangelism spiritual gene strategically nurtured in every cell. This gene causes us to be out-reaching, not just in-reaching, to apply practically the principles of reaching our city person by person, home by home, neighborhood by neighborhood.

Our foremost responsibility as spiritual leaders is to transform our churches to reach cities. Do not allow discouragement or pastoral burnout to hinder God's vision for your church to become the dynamic ministry center it is called to be. The Lord has promised He would build the Church, and we are His helpers.

The Church is the city of the king; it is the royal city. The Church is not meant to be the cast down, miserable and despised, but rather the royal people of God (see Ps. 48:1,2; Zech. 2:8; Heb. 12:22).

Our heavenly citizenship carries the right and obligation to worship our eternal city's one and only God. And we carry His authority and power to loose those who have been forced by sin's grip to live outside the walls. Let us bring them in to the royal city.

House of Prayer
By Sharon Damazio

In this house of prayer,
I come before You now,
Lifting my eyes to You,
Laying my burdens down.
And You will hear my prayer
As I'm calling out to You.
Touch me, Lord, in this house of prayer.

You have always been so faithful.
And I know Your Word is ever true.
When I stand in need,
Your mercy reaches me.
Here I am, calling on Your name again;
Here I am, calling on Your name again.[3]

PERSONAL APPLICATION

1. When was the last time you gave your ministry a spiritual checkup, an evaluation to ensure that your ministry is symptom free of the nine diseases described by Peter Wagner? Early detection could save your ministry.

2. As leaders, we are called to disciple through example. Are you going before the Lord to be "flayed" or inspected? Are you in an accountability group?

3. What are you presenting to your city in your public services? Do the unchurched in your city consider the church living or dead, relevant or irrelevant, legalistic or free? How would the unchurched in your city describe your church if they had to make an evaluation based on your corporate meetings?

Notes
1. Roger S. Greenway, *Discipling the City* (Grand Rapids: Baker Book House, 1992), p. 247.
2. C. Peter Wagner, *The Healthy Church* (Ventura, CA: Regal 1996), pp. 26, 43, 57, 58, 74, 91, 119, 135.
3. Sharon Damazio, "House of Prayer," City Bible Music, 1997. Used with permission.

CHAPTER 10

TRANSFORMING
HOMES INTO
MINISTRY
CENTERS

I kept back nothing that was helpful, but
proclaimed it to you, and taught you publicly and
from house to house.

ACTS 20:20

The Joshua Model has been our point of reference thus far. From the beginning of Joshua's transition into the leadership role passed on by Moses to the crossing of the River Jordan and the taking of Jericho, we have extracted city-reaching principles. We have endeavored to understand what a city securely shut up means to us in the twenty-first century. We have discovered that a city securely shut up can be surprisingly opened by using the right spiritual keys.

These keys have been given to the Church in the city—not one single church, but one collective Church. For the Church in the city to reach a city, it must be spiritually healthy, alive, pulsating with the power and presence of Christ. Cold, stoic, spiritually dead, irrelevant, lukewarm churches will not impact the city—not now, not ever. The power of city reaching is found in the building of a New Testament church, a church with specific, discernible and essential biblical priorities and patterns.

The city-reaching church builds carefully and strategically, believing that the clear models seen in Scripture are the best models to follow. The Jerusalem church in Acts 1—7 and the Antioch church in Acts 11—14 are two of these proven models. Transforming churches to reach cities involves transforming believers' homes to reach neighborhoods. The New Testament shapes our strategy, our convictions, our priorities, our patterns of approach to evangelism, discipling, church planting and world missions.

PAUL, A CITY-REACHING LEADER

The apostle Paul was probably the greatest city-reaching apostle in the New Testament, although he was not alone in his city-reaching vision and ministry. Before Paul's conversion, the believers had already carried the gospel to Jewish communities in various Greco-Roman cities. The church planting that occurred in Antioch was founded by laypeople, natives of Cyprus and Cyrene, who had been forced to leave Jerusalem because of persecution. This Antioch church began an important chapter in the story of Christianity, the beginning of the mother church of the Gentile movement (see Acts 11:19-26).

Paul was a city person through and through; the city breathes through all his Epistles, his language, his metaphors. When Paul cataloged the places where he had suffered danger, he divided the world into cities, wilderness and sea. From his conversion until his death, Paul was given to the city (see Acts 9:6; 28:31). His city-reaching approach was basically family centered; it began most of the time in someone's home. Paul continually used the household-evangelism approach; households were the extended families (see Acts 16:13; 1 Cor. 1:16; Gal. 6:10).

The Greek word for household is *oikos* or *oikia* and designates the social unit that was best fitted for extending the gospel message. The *oikos* household was composed not only of members of the family, but also employees, slaves, tenants and other dependents. This *oikos* approach was the New Testament method Paul and other city reachers used in reaching entire cities for Christ. When Peter went by revelation to Cornelius's household, the Holy Spirit fell, and they were all baptized (see Acts 10:2,48).

To the trembling jailer at Philippi, Paul said, "Believe on the Lord Jesus Christ, and you will be saved, you and your household" (Acts 16:31), and that night "he and all his family were baptized" (v. 33). At Thessalonica, it was Jason and his household (see Acts 17:5-9). At Corinth, Crispus, the leader of the local synagogue, called on the name of the Lord and was baptized along with his household (see Acts 18:8). When Titus Justus, a Gentile, opened his home, Paul preached to the Gentiles (see Acts 18:7).

The household approach to city reaching is certainly a New Testament model and one that will work mightily in the twenty-first century. Paul's city-reaching approach involved laypeople and the home, or the household. In Romans 16, Paul lists his many coworkers in Christ; these were people who, for the most part, opened their homes. Their homes became houses of Holy Spirit activity—what I call "ministry centers."

In cities, people crave the kind of fellowship and interpersonal relationships offered by the church. Therefore, the home must become the powerful ministry center we find in the Early Church:

So continuing daily with one accord in the temple, and breaking bread from house to house, they ate their food with gladness and simplicity of heart, praising God and having favor with all the people. And the Lord added to the church daily those who were being saved (Acts 2:46,47).

LEARNING TO USE OUR HOMES AS MINISTRY CENTERS

The natural progression of developing a ministry perspective involves at least four steps:

1. Your soul becomes a ministry center dispensing Christ from your personal private inner treasury.
2. Your dwelling place, your home, becomes a ministry center dispensing daily the kingdom of God: love, sacrifice, forgiveness, hope, hospitality, healing and the gospel.
3. Your neighborhood and immediate areas become your responsibility for ministry. You gain a vision for your neighbors, neighborhoods, local schools and needy people within your sphere of influence and strategize with others in your household team (cell) to minister to those needs.
4. Your city and metro areas become your larger area of spiritual responsibility. By identifying with and committing to a city-reaching local church, your vision is enlarged to intercede for and work together with the larger Body of Christ to impact the whole city.

And daily in the temple, and in *every house*, they did not cease teaching and preaching Jesus as the Christ (Acts 5:42, italics added).

We believe that home-ministry centers are the most perfectly suited means for reaching this lonely, too busy, relationally starved generation. The city-reaching church must develop this city-reaching model, using the home as a powerful center of Holy Spirit activity. Believe it or not, your home could be the scene of divine surgery where the cutting power of God's Word is used to penetrate spiritual tissue.

CATCH THE VISION

Catching the vision of what God might do through your home is a step in the right direction. John Wesley, the great preacher and founder of the Methodist church, caught the vision from his mother and met the enormous need for outreach, teaching, ministry and leadership in his city with virtually no ordained clergy at his disposal. He enlisted gifted laypeople and started a movement.

As an impressionable boy, John Wesley had observed the undeniable power of the growing Sunday evening ministry of his own mother, Susanna Wesley, while nearly 200 people assembled in and outside her Epworth kitchen. Her example convinced John that laypeople and homes were ideal places of ministry.

There is no place like home, even when the home is someone else's. Homes are practically suited for all aspects of prayer, fellowship, food, privacy, intimacy and accessibility. New people are more comfortable being invited into a home than being invited into a larger church building.

We must begin by removing the fear factor and the "I'm not trained, not capable, not worthy to open my home" mind-set. I suggest that you write 1 Corinthians 1:26-29 on a sheet of paper and pin it up somewhere in your home. Quote it. Sing it. Memorize it:

For you see your calling, brethren, that not many wise according to the flesh, not many mighty, not many noble, are called. But God has chosen the foolish things of the world to put to shame the wise, and God has chosen the weak things of the world to put to shame the things which are mighty; and the base things of the world and the things which are despised God has chosen, and the things which are not, to bring to nothing the things that are, that no flesh should glory in His presence.

You are called. You are more than qualified!

ADJUSTING YOUR LIFE PHILOSOPHY

After you catch the vision, you must also adjust your life philosophy from the American life philosophy to the kingdom of God philosophy. This philosophy gap could be one of the greatest obstacles to making our homes ministry centers. The late Francis Schaffer, historian and philosopher, sheds light on the American problem:

> As the more Christian-dominated consensus weakened, the majority of the people adopted two impoverished values: personal peace and affluence. Personal peace means just to be let alone, not to be troubled by the troubles of other people, whether across the world or across the city. To live one's life with minimal possibilities of being personally disturbed. Personal peace means wanting to have my personal life pattern undisturbed in my lifetime, regardless of what the result will be in the lifetimes of my children and grandchildren. Affluence means an overwhelming and ever-increasing prosperity—a life made up

of things, things and more things—a success judged by ever higher levels of material abundance.[1]

This American philosophical view of life breeds selfishness, isolation, an unreal view of the world around us, pessimism and negativism. A whole generation has been indoctrinated with an endless stream of this "he who has the most toys wins" hedonistic mind-set from birth through college and now they suffer the consequences. George Barna confirms our cultural problems in his book *Virtual America*:

> Almost two thirds of all adults believe life is too complex these days: one out of every six people agreed that sometimes it feels like life is not worth living; three out of every five adults (61%) agreed that the main purpose of life is enjoyment and personal fulfillment. What may be most disturbing about this finding is that half of all born-again Christians and more than one third of all Evangelicals believe that life's purpose is enjoyment and self-satisfaction. Three fourths of all adults agreed that there is no such thing as absolute truth, two people could define truth in totally conflicting ways, but both could still be correct. A similar percentage claim that when it comes to morals and ethics, there are no absolute standards that apply to everybody in all situations. The most desirable attributes for life in the future were identifiable as good health, a clear purpose for living, close friends, a close relationship to God and a comfortable lifestyle.[2]

A generation has been philosophically brainwashed to believe that they should live for themselves, that convenience is desirable above all else, and that entertainment and leisure time are to be coveted. This is a generation that, like no other, needs the gospel message and needs to observe sacrificial living, living for something beyond this temporal life, beyond self-satisfaction and pleasure.

FROM SELF-SERVING TO CITY-SERVING

Reaching our cities begins with allowing Christ to reach our personal worlds, to reach into our lifestyles and ultimately to be Lord over all that we are and all that we have. Reaching cities is a great dream, an inspirational message when preached. People may clap, shout, stand, weep and, in their minds, commit. But then, reality sets in. Reality always has the last word on every subject.

There will be no city reaching without serving, sacrificing, giving up some free time, being inconvenienced by people, involving ourselves in our neighborhoods and opening our homes to the broken lives that need a true healing atmosphere. For our homes to become ministry centers, hosting small groups of praying people, counseling, providing hospitality and teaching the Word, we must be delivered from old-fashioned selfishness and materialistic American dreams. We must make a lifestyle change. The kingdom of God philosophy of life is not complicated, it is not beyond our intellectual capacity to grasp. As we see from the following verses, it's really quite simple and straightforward:

Then He said to them all, "If anyone desires to come after Me, let him deny himself, and take up his cross daily, and follow Me. For whoever desires to save his life will lose it, but whoever loses his life for My sake will save it. For what profit is it to a man if he gains the whole world, and is himself destroyed or lost? For whoever is ashamed of Me and My words, of him the Son of Man will be ashamed when He comes in His own glory, and in His Father's, and of the holy angels" (Luke 9:23-26).

But Jesus called them to Himself and said, "You know that the rulers of the Gentiles lord it over them, and those who are great exercise authority over them. Yet it shall not be so among you; but whoever desires to become great among you, let him be your servant. And whoever desires to be first among you, let him be your slave—just as the Son of Man did not come to be served, but to serve, and to give His life a ransom for many" (Matt. 20:25-28).

For I am already being poured out as a drink offering, and the time of my departure is at hand. I have fought the good fight, I have finished the race, I have kept the faith. Finally, there is laid up for me the crown of righteousness, which the Lord, the righteous Judge, will give to me on that Day, and not to me only but also to all who have loved His appearing (2 Tim. 4:6-8).

THE MISSION OF THE MINISTRY CENTER

Reaching our cities will require a balanced ministry involving both dynamic corporate gatherings of God's people as well as the equipping and releasing of every household to become a powerful on-site (in the neighborhood, the apartment complex or the dormitory) ministry center. The ministry center is a place where Christ is dispensed by ordinary people who, through God, do extraordinary things. Ministry centers can be one home, one family or the individuals within that home ministering Christ to the neighborhood. The ministry center can be a home that hosts a small group of people praying with dedicated regularity, reaching other homes together, providing children's Bible clubs, teaching adult Bible studies, hosting women's support groups, providing meals to those in a crisis, providing a place to build relationships or launching a group for prayerwalking.

The ministry center is a place where Christ

is dispensed by ordinary people who,

through God, do extraordinary things.

The mission statement for our small-group ministry in our neighborhoods is twofold. Our mission is to care for the believers in our local church who are placed in cells geographically and relationally, and to reach our neighborhoods by making relationships, serving and being a Christ ministry center within the reach of every person in our city.

THE URBAN INNER CITY, AN UNCLAIMED FRONTIER

Reaching the city also involves reaching the urban inner city because 50 percent of the world's population now lives in cities, with the majority living in poverty. The urban poor constitute the largest unclaimed frontier that Christian missions have ever encountered. Their living conditions are largely unseen, except in printed statistics and fund-raising photographs.

How are we going to reach cities if we don't reach the poor? The urban poor face many challenges that the Church in the city could minister effectively to:

- The lack of employment opportunities;
- The scarcity of decent and affordable housing;
- The abandoned children by the millions who live on the streets;
- The elderly in the city without adequate financial, emotional or social support;
- The breakdown of family structures;
- The corruption at all levels of government and society;
- The inadequate public services;
- The school dropouts;
- The increase of drugs, violence and gangs;
- The attitudes of anger, despair and bitterness.

(See Deut. 15:1-11; 24:19-22; Luke 14:12-14; 18:22.)

The Church in the city is responsible to minister to the poor continually. If we take care of poverty but neglect to tell the poor the good news about Jesus Christ, we will have failed our mission. If we preach the gospel to the poor but ignore their miserable plight, we will have failed Christ. The challenge is to do both; it's complicated and frustrating at times (see Acts 2:44-47; 4:32).

APPLYING THE BLOOD OF THE LAMB TO MINISTRY CENTERS

The Old Testament Feast of Passover was celebrated as Israel was delivered from Egypt, the house of bondage (see Exod. 13:2; Josh. 24:17), which took place as the Israelites gathered in their houses with a lamb sacrificed for every house. The very title Passover, translated from the Hebrew, means "a passing over, to pass or to hover over." There is the thought of not only the passing over in judgment of the death angel, but also the thought of hovering over in divine protection. God's intention was that all come to experience "household salvation." The following verses (italics added) clearly show that it was a lamb for a *house*:

> Exodus 12:4 "If the household is too small."
> Exodus 12:4 "Let him and his neighbor next to his *house*."
> Exodus 12:7 "Take some of the blood and put it on the two doorposts and on the lintel of the *houses*."
> Exodus 12:13 "Now the blood shall be a sign for you on the *houses* where you are. And when I see the blood, I will pass over you."
> Exodus 12:22 "None of you shall go out of the door of his *house* until morning."
> Exodus 12:23 "The LORD will pass over the door and not allow the destroyer to come into your *houses* to strike you."
> Exodus 12:27 "It is the Passover sacrifice of the LORD, who passed over the *houses* of the children of Israel in Egypt when He struck the Egyptians and delivered our *households*."

> (See Luke 19:5-10; Gen. 7:1; 18:19; Josh. 24:15; John 4:46-54; Acts 16:15,31; 18:3,8.)

The blood of the symbolic sacrificial lamb had to be sprinkled upon every house; it had to be applied. Our homes as ministry centers must be protected by the faith application of the blood of Jesus. The blood of Christ is powerful in resisting evil forces and in releasing Kingdom power (see Heb. 9:14; 10:29; 11:28; Col. 1:13,14). The house becomes a ministry center with authority in dispensing deliverance, forgiveness, healing and cleansing to those who receive from this dedicated ministry center.

REMOVING THE LEAVEN FROM MINISTRY CENTERS

Preparing the house for prayer, worship and ministry to the sojourner and stranger required the removal of all leaven, a time of cleansing and separation. In the natural, leaven is simply a little bit of sourdough placed in a batch of dough that causes fermentation. Leaven works silently, secretly, gradually and consistently until the whole is leavened. In Scripture, leaven is used symbolically as an evil influence that spreads like an infection. All leaven must be put out of the house (see Matt. 26:17-19; Luke 22:1,2).

> Therefore let us keep the feast, not with old leaven, nor with the leaven of malice and wickedness, but with the unleavened bread of sincerity and truth (1 Cor. 5:8).

Our homes must be cleansed of those things that would hinder or corrupt the dispensing of Christ from our ministry centers. The twenty-first century has certainly provided us with every home gadget for entertainment. The home entertainment center has become the norm in most homes. Besides the modernizing of houses, dozens of books, pictures, cards and magazines could also be leaven to our homes.

The ministry center must become cleansed and separated, not allowing secret or corrupting evil influences to hinder the power and presence of Christ in the home. The television and video machine must be monitored wisely in this liberal age. Television presents a distorted view of life, yet it powerfully influences thinking. According to former advertising executive and author Jerry Mander, television doesn't just give us ideas—it determines how we will see those ideas and remember them in our minds.[3]

Zephaniah 1:12 reads: "And it shall come to pass at that time that I will search Jerusalem with lamps, and punish the men who are settled in complacency, who say in their heart, 'The LORD will not do good, nor will He do evil.'" Let us take the lamp of the Holy Spirit and search our houses, removing all leaven that would hinder our homes from becoming dynamic ministry centers for reaching our cities.

DEDICATING OUR MINISTRY CENTERS TO THE LORD

The Scripture is quite clear about God's desire to see our dwelling places dedicated *to Him* and *for Him*. Our homes should be tools in His hands to use as He so desires. They have been given to us for Kingdom purposes:

> And when a man dedicates his house to be holy to the LORD, then the priest shall set a value for it, whether it is good or bad; as the priest values it, so it shall stand (Lev. 27:14).

Deuteronomy 8:12,14 warns us: "lest—when you have eaten and are full, and have built beautiful houses and dwell in them; and...when your heart is lifted up, and you forget the LORD your God who brought you out of the land of Egypt, from the house of bondage."

If you have traveled anywhere else in the world, you have seen that our nation is blessed beyond measure. We have beautiful cities, beautiful towns and thousands upon thousands of beautiful homes. How did we acquire such beautiful homes? By hard work and saving, planning and many years of sweat and toil—yes—but more importantly, by the blessing and multiplied blessings of God upon our lives. Our homes are a reflection of God's goodness.

We can bar the doors shut, keeping out all

intruders and making our homes more like

museums than warm ministry centers, but

if we do, we will only build our own

kingdoms and not God's.

We can bar the doors shut, keeping out all intruders and making our homes more like museums than warm ministry centers, but if we do, we will only build our own kingdoms and not God's. Our homes are not only meant to be places where we store our earthly valuables, collectibles and family relics, but they should also be open storehouses from which we dispense eternal treasures. We should be using our homes as places where we serve others, heal the broken and give precious things away. Let us build memories the whole family and those in our small-group ministries will never forget. As we build our houses, let us not forget to build the Lord's house as well. Let us be wise as Solomon:

Now it happened at the end of twenty years, when Solomon had built the two houses, the house of the LORD and the king's house (1 Kings 9:10).

The dedication of the house, our ministry center, is in direct proportion to our personal dedication to the Lord. Jonathan Edwards prayed a prayer of dedication that served as a model for every believer:

I claim no right to myself, no right to this understanding, this will, these affections that are in me; neither do I have any right to this body or its members—no right to this tongue, to these hands, feet, ears, or eyes.

I have given myself clear away and not retained anything of my own. I have been to God this morning and told Him I have given myself wholly to Him. I have given every power, so that for the future I claim no right to myself in any respect. I have expressly promised Him, for by His grace I will not fail. I take Him as my whole portion and felicity, looking upon nothing else as any part of my happiness. His law is the constant rule of my obedience.

I will fight with all my might against the world, the flesh, and the devil to the end of my life. I will adhere to the faith of the Gospel, however hazardous and difficult the profession and practice of it may be.

I receive the blessed Spirit as my Teacher, Sanctifier, and only Comforter, and cherish all admonitions to enlighten, purify, confirm, comfort, and assist me. This I have done.

I pray God, for the sake of others, to look upon this as a self-dedication, and receive me as His own. Henceforth, I am not to act in any respect as my own. I shall act as my own if I ever make use of any of my powers to do anything that is not to the glory of God, or to fail to make the glorifying of Him my whole and entire business.

If I murmur in the least at afflictions; if I am in any way uncharitable; if I revenge my own case; if I do anything purely to please myself, or omit anything because it is a great denial; if I trust to myself; if I take any praise for any good which Christ does by me; or if I am in any way proud, I shall act as my own and not God's. I purpose to be absolutely His.[4]

Cultivating a God-Empowering Atmosphere

Every place has what we normally call a "felt atmosphere." You may not be able to put your finger on exactly what causes the atmosphere or how the atmosphere was actually created, but you feel the invisible force of either peace, joy, happiness, faith, love and compassion, or confusion, negativity, anger, hopelessness and depression. You may like it or not like it, find it interesting or annoying, but you are faced with a definite feeling. Every house has a built-in layered atmosphere, a hidden personality so to speak, a presence.

Proverbs speaks of the atmosphere in a house that is influenced by the people and their attitudes:

Better is a dry morsel with quietness, than a house full of feasting with strife (Prov. 17:1).

Better to dwell in a corner of a housetop, than in a house shared with a contentious woman (Prov. 21:9).

Jesus teaches His disciples the power of imparting what they had to the house where they ministered; they could leave something in the house or take it back to themselves:

> If the household is worthy, let your peace come upon it. But if it is not worthy, let your peace return to you (Matt. 10:13).

Atmosphere is a pervading or surrounding influence of spirit, general mood or social environment. Atmosphere is affected by décor, music, art and, of course, people. Our ministry centers must cultivate the kind of atmosphere that draws people in and ministers to people without a word being spoken. The house's atmosphere will be created by the underlying values, convictions and attitudes of the people who live in the house or those who make up the small-group ministry that meets in the house.

Nurturing a positive, godly atmosphere is strengthened by giving the Word of God prominence. Deuteronomy 6:9,11 reads, "You shall write them on the doorposts of your house and on your gates...houses full of all good things." Put the Word of God over your house, literally over the entryways, in the main living areas, in and around where people are reminded of God's Word.

The atmosphere of the house will be deeply affected by establishing the presence of the Lord through prayer and worship. Like Abinadab of old, bring the ark into your house. The Ark of the Covenant was symbolic of the voice and presence of God:

> So they set the ark of God on a new cart, and brought it out of the house of Abinadab, which was on the hill; and Uzzah and Ahio, the sons of Abinadab, drove the new cart. And they brought it out of the house of Abinadab, which was on the hill, accompanying the ark of God; and Ahio went before the ark (2 Sam. 6:3,4).

The ark of the LORD remained in the house of Obed-Edom the Gittite three months. And the LORD blessed Obed-Edom and all his household (2 Sam. 6:11).

Invite the Lord's presence to saturate your dwelling place; your house may then become just like the Ark of the Covenant, a place where God will meet with you and speak with you (see Exod. 25:22; Num. 7:89). When God is in the house, there is an atmosphere of worship, of joy and of hope. God in the house makes the difference! The following verses confirm the fact that when God is in the house, an intentional blessing rests upon it:

The curse of the LORD is on the house of the wicked, but He blesses the home of the just (Prov. 3:33).

The wicked are overthrown and are no more, but the house of the righteous will stand (Prov. 12:7).

In the house of the righteous there is much treasure, but in the revenue of the wicked is trouble (Prov. 15:6).

As we spiritually and practically prepare our houses for becoming ministry centers, we move toward releasing ministry to our neighborhoods strategically. Our ministry centers, called City Cells, are small groups of believers meeting together with a defined purpose. Our City Cells have a twofold purpose: City Cell Life and City Cell Reach. City Cell Life is found in its relationships, the mutual caring of one for another. City Cell Reach is our strategy to reach our neighbors, the geographically defined areas of each cell.

We have purposed to establish each cell as a ministry center dispensing the Christ life: grace, forgiveness, hope and love. The cell becomes a house among houses where the glory of God abides. Houses like that of Abinadab (see 1 Sam. 7:1) and Obed-Edom (see 2 Sam. 6:10), houses with the Ark of the Covenant abiding, the presence, power, grace and forgiveness offered because of the Ark of Glory.

BUILDING HOUSES OF GLORY

The goal is to establish hundreds and thousands of houses as glory centers, places where God abides in a powerful way. The glory of God speaks of His beauty, power, honor and authority. God's glory is His moral beauty and perfection of character, His presence that pervades a place.

Our world was created to be a glory center. The following depicts the order of glory revealed in Scripture:

- The God of glory (see Ps. 63:2).
- The Christ of glory (see Ps. 24:8; John 1:14; 2:11).
- The believer and the glory (see Matt. 7:24-27; Col. 1:27; Heb. 3:1-6).
- The home and the glory (see Josh. 24:14; 2 Sam. 6:10,12; 1 Chron. 11:7).
- The church and the glory (see Eph. 3:21).
- The city and the glory (see 2 Sam. 6:10; Rev. 21:33).
- The earth and the glory (see 1 Chron. 22:5; Hab. 2:14).

The Hebrew words used for "glory" denote things that are weighty, or forceful, having splendor and magnificence. When the Ark of the Covenant was placed in the houses of Abinadab and Obed-Edom, on both occasions these houses were wonderfully blessed, filled and anointed (see 1 Sam. 7:1; 2 Sam. 6:10). The Ark of the Covenant represented to the people a place where

God could abide; His abiding represented power and honor, meaning that something significant would happen.

The Ark of the Covenant had six characteristics that become foundational to houses of glory (see Exod. 40:34; 2 Chron. 5:14; 7:1-3):

- Ark of the Covenant
  Houses that make and keep covenant with God.
- The Mercy Seat
  Houses that receive and dispense the mercy of God.
- Tables of the Law
  Houses that establish standards saturated in love.
- The Manna
  Houses that are faith filled for God's miraculous provision.
- The Rod of Aaron
  Houses that accept God's sovereignty in His choices.
- The Glory of God
  Houses that have a living presence of God.

God is calling the Church to line up with biblical models in the temple and house to house; both the corporate and the house are God's pattern. To build houses of glory that will become dynamic ministry centers in our neighborhoods and throughout our cities, we must catch a vision, work diligently to change our thinking about lifestyle, nurture a spirit of servanthood and sacrifice. We must open our eyes to see our cities the way they really are, not the way they appear to be.

OUR HOMES, LIGHTHOUSES OF PRAYER

Ed Silvoso calls these ministry centers "Lighthouses of Prayer." He says the best way to infiltrate Satan's perimeter in our cities is by turning every Christian home into a prayer cell. Prayer cells must be established throughout the city so that no neighborhood is left without a spiritual lighthouse.

Our church members should be organized into neighborhood prayer cells until every block in the city is being prayed for. In this manner, we will be deploying the largest number of troops possible with the least possible logistical disruption to inflict the greatest possible damage upon the enemy with a minimum possible risk.[5]

The goal of establishing home ministry centers is to penetrate the enemy's territory in a systematic manner. George Otis, Jr. defines the three stages of moving toward community transformation as follows:[6]

1. Establishing spiritual beachheads, an initial phase where revived believers enter into united prayer.
2. Spiritual breakthrough, a subsequent interval characterized by rapid and substantial church growth.
3. A spiritual transformation, a climatic season attended by dramatic sociopolitical renewal.

The establishing of homes as ministry centers is the establishing of spiritual beachheads. Each cell becomes a small attacking army unit under the greater covering of the local church. It becomes the behind-enemy-lines forces. Prayer intercession, good deeds, prayerwalking, spiritual warfare, power encounters—all these become the function of ministry centers.

Some of our greatest challenges and spiritual oppositions have occurred when seeking to establish our home ministry centers as spiritual beachheads. Whenever the Church moves toward the city, toward ministering to the unsaved through prayer and preaching, the enemy immediately counterattacks. His desire is to keep the Church playing church, existing but not forcefully taking ground. He tries to blind the Church vision to the harvest that is ripe and ready to be picked; he does this by frustrating believers, hammering them with attacks upon their health, finances, relationships and spiritual fervor.

Our home ministry centers see these acts of retaliation clearly and respond by adding more intercessory prayer, more corporate prayer with fasting, and more leadership unity and protection for one another. We are not ignorant of Satan's devices, nor are we presumptuous to ignore his attacks. Our ministry centers have a clear purpose, and we are pursuing this purpose diligently.

MINISTRY CENTERS MINISTERING THE LIFE OF CHRIST

The following verses provide a framework for the purposes and promises of homes that become God's city-reaching ministry centers:

HOUSES OF HEALING

Now when Jesus had come into Peter's house, He saw his wife's mother lying sick with a fever. So He touched her hand, and the fever left her. And she arose and served them (Matt. 8:14,15).

And when He had come into the house, the blind men came to Him. And Jesus said to them, "Do you believe that I am able to do this?" They said to Him, "Yes, Lord" (Matt. 9:28).

And again He entered Capernaum after some days, and it was heard that He was in the house (Mark 2:1).

When He came into the house, He permitted no one to go in except Peter, James, and John, and the father and mother of the girl (Luke 8:51).

HOUSES OPEN TO ALL

Now it happened, as Jesus sat at the table in the house, that behold, many tax collectors and sinners came and sat down with Him and His disciples (Matt. 9:10).

So that servant came and reported these things to his master. Then the master of the house, being angry, said to his servant, "Go out quickly into the streets and lanes of the city, and bring in here the poor and the maimed and the lame and the blind." And the servant said, "Master, it is done as you commanded, and still there is room." Then the master said to the servant, "Go out into the highways and hedges, and compel them to come in, that my house may be filled" (Luke 14:21-23).

And when Jesus was in Bethany at the house of Simon the leper (Matt. 26:6).

HOUSES OF DELIVERANCE

And when she had come to her house, she found the demon gone out, and her daughter lying on the bed (Mark 7:30).

Behold, I give you the authority to trample on serpents and scorpions, and over all the power of the enemy, and nothing shall by any means hurt you (Luke 10:19).

Or how can one enter a strong man's house and plunder his goods, unless he first binds the strong man? And then he will plunder his house (Matt. 12:29).

HOUSES OF SALVATION

And when Jesus came to the place, He looked up and saw him, and said to him, "Zacchaeus, make haste and come down, for today I must stay at your house" (Luke 19:5).

And Jesus said to him, "Today salvation has come to this house, because he also is a son of Abraham" (Luke 19:9).

HOUSES WITH HOLY SPIRIT ACTIVITY

And suddenly there came a sound from heaven, as of a rushing mighty wind, and it filled the whole house where they were sitting (Acts 2:2).

HOUSES OF HOSPITALITY

And when she and her household were baptized, she begged us, saying, "If you have judged me to be faithful to the Lord, come to my house and stay." So she persuaded us (Acts 16:15).

Then they spoke the word of the Lord to him and to all who were in his house. And he took them the same hour of the night and washed their stripes. And immediately he and all his family were baptized. Now when he had brought them into his house, he set food before them; and he rejoiced, having believed in God with all his household (Acts 16:32-34).

So they went out of the prison and entered the house of Lydia; and when they had seen the brethren, they encouraged them and departed (Acts 16:40).

HOUSES OF EVANGELISM

And he departed from there and entered the house of a certain man named Justus, one who worshiped God, whose house was next door to the synagogue. Then Crispus, the ruler of the synagogue, believed on the Lord with all his household. And many of the Corinthians, hearing, believed and were baptized (Acts 18:7,8).

On the next day we who were Paul's companions departed and came to Caesarea, and entered the house of Philip the evangelist, who was one of the seven, and stayed with him (Acts 21:8).

As we move into city-reaching strategies, God desires city-reaching homes—homes where He can bring His ark and abide, homes that will make covenant, dispense mercy, establish standards, homes where faith is the force and God is the center, where people enter and say, "Surely the Lord is in this place, and I did not know it" (Gen. 28:16).

It's Not By Might
By Sharon Damazio

"It's not by might, it's not by power
But by my Spirit," says the Lord.
"It's not by might, it's not by power
But by my Spirit," says the Lord.

You did not choose the wise.
You did not choose the noble.
You did not choose the mighty or the strong.
But You went to the field of the broken
And You looked for a vessel of clay;
For the one who would wholly surrender;
For the one who would trust and obey.

I stand amazed at the mighty things You've done.
I need more of Your Spirit, more of Your grace
To finish the work You've begun.[7]

PERSONAL APPLICATION

1. The urban poor constitute the largest unclaimed frontier for Christian missions. What are you as a leader doing to impact the inner city for Christ?

2. Today, more than ever, we are faced with bringing leaven into our homes through various forms of media. How much time do you spend in front of the television? Has entertainment caused you to become complacent about God's agenda for reaching your neighborhood or city?

3. Does your home have a positive, godly atmosphere? Do your family members and neighbors experience the Ark of the Covenant there? Have you written God's Word upon the doorposts and entryways?

4. Your home is called to be a lighthouse of prayer. How much time do you spend praying for your neighbors? Do your neighbors think of your home as a place where the glory of God is manifested? If not, write out some steps you will begin to take to change.

Notes
1. Francis Schaeffer, *How Then Should We Live* (Old Tappan, N.J.: Fleming H. Revell Company, 1976), p. 205.
2. George Barna, *Virtual America* (Ventura, CA: Regal Books, 1994), p. 76.
3. Kenneth Gangel and James Wilholt, *Handbook on Family Life Education* (Grand Rapids: Baker Book House, 1996), pp. 246, 247.
4. Paul Lee Tan, *Encyclopedia of 7,700 Illustrations* (Rockville, MD: Assurance Publishers, 1979), p. 270.

5. Ed Silvoso, *That None Should Perish* (Ventura, CA: Regal Books, 1994), p. 254.
6. George Otis, Jr., *Informed Intercession* (Ventura, CA: Regal Books, 1998), p. 4.
7. Sharon Damazio, "It's Not By Might," City Bible Music, 1998. Used with permission.

CHAPTER 11

SECURING
BORDERS AND RECLAIMING
OUR CITIES

*We have a strong city; God makes salvation
its walls and ramparts.*

ISAIAH 26:1

The transformed church becomes a vehicle for revival and restoration both in believers' and unbelievers' worlds. A transformed church is lifted out of its self-centered spirituality, a mentality that says we are victims rather than victorious. The transformed church has a definite vision for the city, a vision to reach the city and make it a place where God's presence, God's ways and God's Word are powerful forces felt by all in the city. Our cities have a definite God-purpose to be fulfilled, a purpose that will only be fulfilled if the church will become a city-reaching church.

Most cities worldwide are filled with violence, drugs, gangs, prostitution, poverty and perversion, but this is not God's intention for these cities. And yet God works through faith. Therefore we must ask ourselves: What do we expect God to do in our cities? Is our vision too small? Too big? God will be to us only as big as what we expect of Him in time and space. We must begin to claim biblical promises and preach biblical hope if we are to expect biblical results. The city will be effectively influenced by the power of the gospel because the city is people, and people can be and will be reached either by the kingdom of God or the kingdom of Satan.

Our strategy must be one birthed in the spiritual realm and implemented strategically by spiritual means; natural carnal means will not accomplish spiritual ends. We must reach our cities by understanding the spiritual realm. First the spiritual, then the natural. First we take our territory by spiritual invasion, then through natural channels. As this happens, the trans-formed church begins to think like and function like a New Testament church. The transformed homes begin to think like and function like homes with a purpose, reaching every person with the gospel of Christ.

PRAYER, OUR SPIRITUAL FIREPOWER

One of the first steps to establishing a city-reaching church atmosphere is to establish a prayer intercession priority in the church, in every believer and, ultimately, in the whole City Church. Prayer intercession for the city will grow out of a prayer spirit that is nurtured and strengthened continually within each local congregation. To think that we have any chance at all to touch our cities without becoming powerful in prayer is ludi-crous. Our prayer power will be the power that breaks down the spiritual strongholds in our churches, then in our cities. We will not be spiritually able to secure the borders of our cities until we can secure the borders in our own congregations. George Otis, Jr. explains:

> The second core factor in community transformation is fervent, united prayer. In each of our featured case studies, breakthroughs occurred when intercessors addressed specific concerns in common cause. Many of these group efforts took on their own unique identities. In Cali, Columbia, 60,000 intercessors held all-night vigils and circled the city in mobile prayer caravans. In Kampala, Uganda, hand-holding prayer warriors referred to their daily disciples as the wailing wall. In Kiambu, Kenya, believers petitioned God from a store basement that they dubbed the prayer care. Their successes led to subsequent intercessory campaigns such as Morning Glory and Operation Prayer Storm.[1]

The power for spiritually penetrating the darkness in our cities is the power of red-hot intercessory prayer.

OUR CHURCH'S INTERCESSORY PRAYER PILGRIMAGE

As our church moved toward a clearer vision for our city, my first assignment from the Lord was to build a greater firepower of prayer. This I systematically set out to accomplish through teaching and equipping our church in every level of prayer that I could discern from Scripture.

The first level was personal prayer. Again, before we go to war against city principalities, we should be trained in the discipline of personally touching God through prayer. We took Hosea 10:12 as our prayer text and spent many weeks going through each word:

Sow for yourselves righteousness; reap in mercy; break up your fallow ground, for it is time to seek the LORD, till He comes and rains righteousness on you.

The series was titled "The Seven Power Points of Prayer," and our goal was to build a stronger, deeper, more powerfully alive personal prayer life in the congregation before we set out to build prayer intercession for the city. We prayed Saint Augustine's prayer as our hearts' cry:

Oh Lord, the house of my soul is narrow, enlarge it, that You may enter in. I confess it, I know, but what shall cleanse it, to whom shall I cry out but to You? Cleanse me from my secret faults, Oh Lord, and spare Your servant from strange sins.[2]

Our desire was to enlarge the soul of each individual through prayer, desiring to enflame the passions of the heart for prayer, teaching the church to break up the fallow ground of the heart, plow it and sow it with a prayer spirit.

THE SEVEN POWER POINTS OF PRAYER

We used the following outline for "The Seven Power Points of Prayer" based on Hosea 10:12:

1. The Preparation of Prayer—*"Break up"*
   Prayer begins with a heart and mind that have been softened and planted with the Word of God. "Breaking up" the soil of our hearts refers to a personal commitment to confession and repentance.
2. The Hindrances of Prayer—*"Fallow ground"*
   The condition of our hearts determines our growth,

our fruitfulness and our destinies in God. Even as there are different conditions of physical soil, so there are different heart conditions that must be discerned in order to bring forth great fruitfulness in the spiritual realm.

3. The Urgency of Prayer—*"For it is time"*
   We live in the glorious "now" of God. The whole of time is God's arena to work on behalf of and through His faithful ones. He desires that His people be mighty in prayer, experienced in getting answers to prayer and undisturbed by the most complex or long-standing needs.

4. The Focus of Prayer—*"To seek the Lord"*
   It is time to seek the Lord. Seeking prayer is an earnest, continual perseverance birthed from a deep hunger and drive. Seeking prayer is prayer that is Holy Spirit initiated and, through intercession, finds God's will and God's answers.

5. The Persistence of Prayer—*"Till"*
   Many prayers are granted by God but given up by the ones praying because they stopped praying before the answer came. Without the dynamic of persistence, much prayer remains unanswered.

6. The Dynamic Presence of Christ in Prayer—*"He comes"*
   Power in prayer comes from the empowering of the Holy Spirit within us. As we use that power in prayer, He continues to empower us for prayer and breathe His Spirit in us.

7. The Abundant Answers to Prayer—*"Rains righteousness on you"*
   The rain of God is symbolic of God's favor, blessings, strength and prosperity. It is prayer that both releases the rain of God and allows us to receive the rain of God.

Prayer is a vital, essential part of preparing a city-reaching church. Prayer is vital to all God's people for the advancement of the Kingdom. All the congregations must become skilled if we are to spiritually change the climate of the city. God desires all of us to be mighty in prayer, experienced in receiving answered prayer and unmoved in persevering in the most complex or long-standing needs. As we can see from the following verses, when this holy, fervent flame of prayer is lit, the soul awakens to the interest of heaven, attracts the attention of God and places at the disposal of those who exercise it the exhaustless riches of grace:

> Let us therefore come boldly to the throne of grace, that we may obtain mercy and find grace to help in time of need (Heb. 4:16).

> Let my prayer be set before You as incense, the lifting up of my hands as the evening sacrifice (Ps. 141:2).

> One thing I have desired of the Lord, that will I seek: that I may dwell in the house of the LORD all the days of my life, to behold the beauty of the LORD, and to inquire in His temple (Ps. 27:4).

OPENING-SERVICE INTERCESSION

We at City Bible Church established a prayer focus that encouraged a new level of prayer in each individual believer and then raised the level of corporate prayer. For many years, prior to every service, we had what we called "Pre-Service Prayer," a 30-minute corporate prayer time in a room other than our sanctuary. This corporate prayer time had been successful in keeping a prayer focus, but not everyone was consistently committed to coming one-half hour before the service.

To further our prayer atmosphere goal, we moved the prayer time into the sanctuary at the beginning of each service, calling it "Opening Service Intercession." Our goal was to expose the entire congregation on a weekly basis to the power of prayer intercession. This was accomplished through a 12-month preaching focus on intercessory prayer based on Ezekiel 22:30:

> So I sought for a man among them who would make a wall, and stand in the gap before Me on behalf of the land, that I should not destroy it; but I found no one.

The series was entitled "Gap Standing and Hedge Building: Responding to the Call of the Spirit to Become a Church of Intercession." Our goal was to motivate the entire congregation into a deeper level of prayer intercession that would release the supernatural power of God in an obvious and awesome manner, resulting in awesome harvest.

Intercessory prayer is the single most important

of all ministries in the Church.

First, we established the power of personal prayer (see Hosea 10:12), then the power of corporate prayer (see Ezek. 22:30). Believing that the whole congregation is called to participate in prayer intercession and go deeper, to learn more and to become skilled intercessors, we preached and modeled intercession during every service.

Intercessory prayer is the single most important of all ministries in the Church. Prayer creates an expectant, heavenly-charged atmosphere and binds the power of darkness so the gospel can go forward and the Church can prosper. Intercessory prayer is the sign of a person's soul expanding, deepening and becoming like Christ in compassion and mercy. Without intercessory prayer, the protective hedge around our borders may be broken down, allowing easy access for the enemy to come in to destroy people, homes, marriages, families, spiritual life and health both in our churches and our cities. Corporate intercessory prayer has incredible power to change "what is" to "what can be" by the power and grace of God, in spite of whatever obstacles appear to be hindering the Church (see Exod. 8:28; Isa. 59:16; Jer. 27:18; Rev. 5:8; 8:3,4).

OUR PRAYER SEQUENCE

We established a prayer sequence, prayer in the house—open heavens over the city. The prayer sequence is:

Interceding Leaders

▽

Interceding People

▽

Interceding Atmosphere

▽

Interceding Churches

▽

Interceding Principles and Warfare

▽

Interceding for Cities and Nations

As you can see, you don't start with cities and nations first. You must first establish power and momentum before taking on

the city. After we nurtured a new level of general prayer intercession, we then established a specialized intercession level. The
whole church becomes a prayer intercession instrument and then
special focus areas are taken on by the specialized intercessors.
We have a seven-day-a-week Prayer Center (as of this writing,
there are more than 2,000 churches with Prayer Centers), a Prayer
Pastor, a Prayer Center Overseer, Prayer Teams for every staff pastor, Prayer Teams for each service, prayer during the service and a
variety of prayer teams. The following list provides a more
detailed, but not complete, picture of our prayer foundation:

- **Ministry Team Intercessors:** Intercessors who minister
  during services at altar calls, over water baptism candidates and pray for healing and urgent needs. These
  intercessors must be approved by an elder or pastor
  and function with the laying on of hands.
- **Service Intercessors:** A scheduled core of intercessors—
  but open to any intercessor—who meet during the
  Sunday morning service behind the stage, with audio-
  visual reception of the service. Prayer focuses on that
  Sunday's message.
- **Third Row Intercessors:** Scheduled intercessors sit in
  the third row behind the pastors' pew during all services. Throughout the service they focus on praying for
  me, my family, the MC and guest speakers.
- **Pre-Service Soaking Prayer:** Open to anyone interested
  in receiving soaking prayer prior to the Sunday evening
  service. Ministry Team Intercessors are available to
  soak anyone desiring prayer, such as visiting ministry,
  worship teams, water baptismal candidates, STORM
  Teams, et cetera. Two or three intercessors also pray
  over every seat in the sanctuary.

- **Event Engine Room Intercessors:** Intercessors who meet backstage to pray prior to and during special events, such as the Eternity Production, conference, retreats, et cetera.
- **Event Intercessors:** Intercessors who pray in their homes for the participants in special events, such as the Eternity Production, STORM Teams, Tapestry Teams, conferences and children's productions, before, during and after the event.
- **City Care Prayer Warriors:** Intercessors who pray in their homes receive weekly prayer lists taken from the pew information cards and pray for City Bible Church (CBC) visitors, their prayer requests and CBC members' prayer requests.
- **Departmental Armor Bearers:** Intercessors who are assigned to cover different departments throughout CBC. They pray in their homes and meet at specific times in the Prayer Center to pray with members of those departments.
- **Healing Prayer:** Intercessors and those needing physical healing meet in the Prayer Center weekly for a brief time of teaching before praying for the sick.
- **Daniel Prayer Intercessors:** Intercessors who meet in the Prayer Center to intercede specifically for spiritual breakthrough in our city, state and nation.
- **Deborahs Arise:** Intercessors who meet in our Prayer Center to pray for our prodigals.
- **Personal Armor Bearers:** Intercessors who are a part of specific teams chosen by elders and department heads to pray for them, their families and ministries. The intercessors pray in their homes and meet at specific times to pray for their leaders with the laying on of hands.

- **Prayer Guard:** Intercessors who pray daily in their homes at a secondary level for leaders, their families and ministries as assigned. They do not meet with the leader.
- **Threefold Cord Intercessors:** Intercessory groups, consisting of three individuals or three couples, who agree to pray together for one another on a consistent basis.
- **Downtown Intercessors:** Intercessors who meet weekly downtown in the Justice Center to pray and praywalk the business and city government districts.
- **Strategic City Taking Intercessors:** Intercessors who meet on Friday evening for Spirit-led "times of war" with prayer that is focused on Portland and Vancouver.
- **Pray Portland:** CBC hosts an hour-long program every Sunday morning from 6:00 to 7:00 A.M. on KKSL Radio. Teams of eight intercessors pray for the City of Portland on the air consecutively for 60 minutes.
- **Northwest Prayer Watch:** Intercessors who meet in the Prayer Center to pray for the harvest and prayer requests from the churches of the Northwest: Oregon, Washington and Idaho.

Our broad foundation of praying people allows us to focus on the city with prayer intercession that cannot be intimidated, outflanked or counterattacked without knowing what's happening. We are more prepared for a wider variety of spiritual warfare because we are more broadly equipped. Our Opening Service Intercession involves prayer for personal cleansing, personal enlargement, renewal of the heart, Holy Spirit empowerment and prayer for our city. We pray against specific spiritual strongholds in our region; we pray for the lost; and we pray for revival. This opening intercession will last about 20 minutes and flows into a worship time. (I discuss the whole topic of prayer intercession individually, corporately and for our cities in my book *Seasons of Intercession*.[3])

ESTABLISHING GOD'S PERIMETERS

The prayer anointing is absolutely essential to reaching our cities by tearing down spiritual strongholds, piercing the darkness and setting the captives free. Realizing that our city was notorious for New Age material, pornography, euthanasia, legalizing medical marijuana, worshiping mother earth and several other obvious strongholds, we decided to spiritually claim our borders.

Ed Silvoso says that the first step to reaching an entire city for Christ is to establish God's perimeters in the city. In military science a perimeter is the outer boundary of an area where defenses are set up. The term implies a warfare context, real or potential.[4] I would say the warfare is real! That's one very good reason why you need prayer power before you start assaulting the enemy.

When we moved toward a strategy to reach our city, we moved into another level of spiritually intense warfare. It was January 2, 1998 when we launched our first staking of the borders of our city. We chose to stake out the Northeast/Southeast section of our city that represented more than 800,000 of our 1.5 million metro area population. I asked several pastors in our city with whom we have a relationship and who are representative of a broad section of the City Church in the Northeast and Southeast areas to join with us.

Baptist, Independent, Evangelical, Pentecostal, Charismatic and Foursquare pastors were involved—Caucasian, African-American and Hispanic. Together we set out to do what we simply called Reclaiming Our Borders, a spiritual proclamation. We mapped out our route and made wooden stakes with appropriate

Scriptures written on each one of them. Then we set out to claim our borders in three vans. The first van was packed with pastors, the second and third van were filled with very noisy intercessors. The scriptures we put on the stakes were Psalms 46:1-5; 48:2,3; 68:3-11; 107:6-8; Proverbs 11:11; Isaiah 1:26; 26:1-7; 33:20,21; 54:2-5; 58:11,12; 62:11,12; Matthew 16:16-19; Acts 18:9,10. We claimed the following border scriptures:

> David also defeated Hadadezer the son of Rehob, king of Zobah, as he went to recover his territory at the River Euphrates (2 Sam. 8:3).

> The lines have fallen to me in pleasant places; yes, I have a good inheritance (Ps. 16:6).

> You have set all the borders of the earth; you have made summer and winter (Ps. 74:17).

> And He brought them to His holy border, this mountain which His right hand had acquired. He also drove out the nations before them, allotted them an inheritance by survey, and made the tribes of Israel dwell in their tents (Ps. 78:54,55).

> He makes peace in your borders, and fills you with the finest wheat (Ps. 147:14).

> Even though Edom has said, "We have been impoverished, but we will return and build the desolate places," thus says the Lord of hosts: "They may build, but I will throw down; they shall be called the Territory of Wickedness, and the people against whom the LORD will have indignation forever" (Mal. 1:4).

As we moved to each premarked staking spot, the van of intercessors followed and sustained continuous intercession during the whole event, about five hours in length. At each spot we gathered around the stake and read a prayer proclamation, then each pastor took a turn with the sledgehammer to drive the stake in the ground. Finally, we poured oil upon it, placed our feet on top of the stake and prayed for our city borders to be reclaimed.

OUR PRAYER PROCLAMATION

The prayer proclamation I wrote for the occasion is as follows:

On the basis of Scripture, we as leaders stand in the gap for our city. We pastors of Northeast and Southeast Portland stand together as representatives of other city leaders who desire to:

Repent (Dan. 9:4-9). We ask the Lord Jesus to forgive us for sins that have taken place in our state, in our city, in our Northeast and Southeast regions. We ask forgiveness for the sins of political corruption, racial prejudice, moral perversions, witchcraft, the occult and idolatry. We pray the blood of Jesus to cleanse our hands from shedding innocent blood in the acts of abortion, euthanasia and any other ways the innocent have been destroyed. We ask forgiveness for divisions in the Church, for spiritual pride, for backbiting, for anything that has hurt the Church of Jesus Christ. We repent, humble ourselves and ask for mercy to be poured out upon our land, our community and our churches.

Request (Jer. 29:7). We ask for God's kingdom to come and His will to be done on earth as it is in heaven. We ask

in the name of the Lord Jesus Christ for a spiritual outpouring of God's grace, mercy and fire upon our city. We
ask for true spiritual revival to come to our community,
causing a turning to God, a cleansing, a brokenness, a
humility, a hunger for the one and only true God. God,
we ask for mercy here. We ask that our destiny not be
aborted. We ask that you visit our city, our churches and
our homes. Do not pass our city by. We ask for restoration
of the foundations of righteousness to our city.

Resist (Eph. 6:10-17; Jas. 4:7). On the basis of our submission to God, we in faith resist the devil and his work.
We resist all forces and powers of evil that have taken
hold of our city. We resist the spirit of wickedness that
has established strongholds in our city region—the dark
places, the hidden works of darkness, the mystery places
where the enemy has set up encampments. We call on
the name of the Lord to destroy all spiritual strongholds. We proclaim this day that the city of Portland,
especially the Northeast and Southeast regions, is now
under the power and ownership of the Holy Spirit. All
other spirits are hereby given notice and are evicted from
this property by the power of the name of Jesus. Today
we stand in the gap and rebuild a hedge of protection
around our city.

We claim this day Isaiah 58:11,12: "The LORD will
guide you continually, and satisfy your soul in drought,
and strengthen your bones; you shall be like a watered garden, and like a spring of water, whose waters do not fail.
Those from among you shall build the old waste places;
you shall raise up the foundations of many generations;

and you shall be called the Repairer of the Breach, the Restorer of Streets to Dwell In."

We claim this day Isaiah 1:26: "I will restore your judges as at the first, and your counselors as at the beginning. Afterward you shall be called the city of righteousness, the faithful city."

We claim this day Matthew 16:18,19: "And I also say to you that you are Peter, and on this rock I will build My church, and the gates of Hades shall not prevail against it. And I will give you the keys of the kingdom of heaven, and whatever you bind on earth will be bound in heaven, and whatever you loose on earth will be loosed in heaven."

Now we pray that our city will be reclaimed, restored, revived and set on a path of righteousness. We pray that our borders will be secured on this day, January 4, 1998. May God give us grace, protect us and allow His angels to encamp round about us. This we do in humility and faith.

IDENTIFICATIONAL REPENTANCE

The President of Zambia, President Chiluba, prayed for his nation with what we would call identificational repentance:

Dear God, as a nation we now come to You, to Your throne of grace, and we humble ourselves and admit our guilt. We repent from all our wicked ways of idolatry, witchcraft, the occult, immorality, injustice, and corruption and other sins that have violated Your righteous laws. We turn away from all this and renounce it all in Jesus' name. We ask for forgiveness and cleansing through the blood of Jesus. Therefore, we thank You that You will heal our land. We pray that You will send healing, restoration, revival, blessing and prosperity to Zambia.[5]

The purpose of staking the city is to geographically proclaim repentance over the city. The church is identifying with the corporate sins of the city, repenting of those sins, forsaking them and publicly apologizing. This may not visibly solve all the problems in the city, and there may be no identifiable changes to the natural eye, but in the spiritual world, we are taking away the places the enemy has a right to invade. We are cleansing things in the invisible realm as Daniel did in Daniel 9:4-19. The sins Daniel identified with were not his personal sins, he did not commit the sins, but he did repent with and for the people. He believed God would do something for the nation if he would confess, repent, weep and ask for cleansing.

John Dawson, a leader in identification repentance, says: "If we have broken our covenant with God and violated our relationships with one another, the path to reconciliation must begin with the act of confession."[6]

Bob Beckett gives more counsel on the subject of identificational repentance: "It is conventional in that we must seek God's forgiveness for personal sin as well as for sin committed by the Church. Without asking His forgiveness, we have no business attempting any kind of spiritual warfare. But the call to repentance is unconventional in that the object of repentance includes much more than the sins for which we as individuals are responsible. The term given to this broader expression of penitence is identificational repentance, an act by which we identify with and ask forgiveness for the sin of a group, a city, or a nation, with which we are connected. Identificational repentance is a powerful weapon in our arsenal of warfare whose time has come."[7]

The principle of identificational repentance for cities and nations is found in Scripture on several occasions—Daniel (see Dan. 9:1-19), Nehemiah (see Neh. 1:4-11), Moses, and Jeremiah—not just from one obscure passage. Jesus uses the term "remitting of sins," meaning to pardon or forgive sin through identifying and speaking words of remittance.

John 20:23 reads: "If you forgive the sins of any, they are forgiven them; if you retain the sins of any, they are retained."

When we staked our city, by faith, we identified with the corporate city sins, racial injustice, worship of other gods, perversions and immorality, and asked God to have mercy on our city by first cleansing the church. Securing the borders may seem unreal to many, down right unscriptural to some, and subjective or just plain nonsense to others. But we believed it would help loosen the principalities and powers that were preventing the gospel from flowing freely into our city. Certainly it didn't hurt anything to spend several hours repenting, interceding and proclaiming Scriptures over our city. The fact that we had more people bowing their knees and asking Christ into their hearts in the following 12 months than at any other time in the history of our local church might be connected to our prayers of repentance and securing our borders.

After staking our city, we met together for a City Church Communion Service with the pastors and some of their congregations at our church facility (our building was the largest) to publicly confess our sins, claim our borders and intercede for our city. Nearly 3,000 people, pastors and city leaders spent three hours in prayer, worship, intercession, confession, repentance and partaking of communion together. We communicated to the congregations with a video of the city staking and a biblical statement explaining why we did this and what we expected.

By prayer staking the geographical boundaries of our city with proclamation and repentance, our City Church was identifying with the corporate sins of Portland, Oregon, and Vancouver, Washington, our metro area, repenting, forsaking and publicly apologizing. These corporate sins included racial hostility toward Native Americans, African-Americans and Asians, sins of immorality, idolatry, occultism and covenant breaking. The Scriptures we read and interceded with had a powerful impact on the event. They are as follows:

> When the Most High divided their inheritance to the nations, when He separated the sons of Adam, he set the boundaries of the peoples according to the number of the children of Israel (Deut. 32:8).

> "For I will restore health to you and heal you of your wounds," says the LORD, "Because they called you an outcast saying: 'This is Zion; no one seeks her'" (Jer. 30:17).

> Declare among the nations, proclaim, and set up a standard; proclaim—do not conceal it—say, "Babylon is taken, Bel is shamed. Merodach is broken in pieces; her idols are humiliated, her images are broken in pieces." For out of the north a nation comes up against her, which shall make her land desolate, and no one shall dwell therein. They shall move, they shall depart, both man and beast (Jer. 50:2,3).

> So I sought for a man among them who would make a wall, and stand in the gap before Me on behalf of the land, that I should not destroy it; but I found no one (Ezek. 22:30).

> For we do not wrestle against flesh and blood, but against principalities, against powers, against the rulers of the darkness of this age, against spiritual hosts of wickedness in the heavenly places (Eph. 6:12).

START WHERE YOU ARE WITH AS MANY AS YOU CAN

Corporate intercession with the City Church pastors, elders, leaders and congregations is a powerful tool for city intercession and city warfare. We only had a seed of representation from our whole metro area.

If you wait until you have a majority it may never happen—you have to start somewhere! It could be the city will have several different groups doing the same things at the same time and maybe in the future the groups will merge for further unified expression. Don't get paralyzed by what Peter Wagner calls hyper-cooperativism. With cooperation being the "in" thing these days, the danger of hyper-cooperativism increases.

In the church cooperation can be useful for some activities in a city or region—social action projects, taking a stand against or for a moral political law such as abortion or euthanasia, et cetera. The local church, however, must be unified with other local churches and local pastors to pray for and do spiritual warfare for the city. And yet this type of ministry may not be accepted by all churches in the city. If you wait to get a majority you may never do some of these things. Start where you are, gather as many as you can—1, 2, 10, 15, 20, and let it grow.

We sponsor City Pastors' Breakfasts three or four times a year with 200 to 250 out of 1,200 pastors in our city attending. The breakfasts are aimed at certain levels of prayer, unity and city focus. We eat, we fellowship, we meet and we introduce new pastors who have pioneered or taken over a church in our city. Then we pray for new pastors, and allow pastors to hand out "city event" communications. Finally, we worship, and usually hear from a visiting speaker. We don't push a certain strategy to reach our city, trying to get everyone on board.

We seek general unity, not specific unity. If we would have asked that group of 250 pastors to come to a place of biblical conviction and spiritual unity in the area of symbolism, spiritual subjectivity, spiritual warfare and identificational repentance, I don't think the city staking would have happened. As a matter of fact, we might still be there discussing it! Within the larger breakfast group, I have reached out to those who seem to have the same vision and ideas for reaching our city. This group only consists of about 20 pastors who meet monthly. We pray together, open up our ministries to one another, preach at each other's churches and help each other in any way we can.

As a local pastor, I found it easy to become spiritually paralyzed with City Church politics, personal agendas, theological debates, and to simply back off and do nothing. I didn't want to be misread, criticized: "He's not with us," or "He's one of those independent churches. You know, they do things on their own." Those fears prevented me from doing the things I had faith for and convictions about. However, as a local pastor, I have a responsibility to pray, repent, confess, claim and reach. I'm doing these things with as many pastors as I can move ahead with, and I still cooperate in larger city events, such as the Billy Graham Crusade, Luis Palau Crusade, City Pastor Prayer Summits and more. I believe every pastor should find those he relates to and do what he can do to reach the city.

The same principle applies to racial reconciliation: I heard it; I did it with others in large conferences and city events, but I didn't personally feel reconciled. I needed to go to another level, so I called one of the African-American pastors in our city, sat down and said, "Teach me to understand why we need to be reconciled. What is it, and how can I change our relationship?" This contact began a series of events that caused racial reconciliation to become a reality for me, the church I pastor and our ministry to the inner city.

With all the books, articles and conferences on city reaching that are available, you have to start somewhere. Prayer intercession with either a small or large group of pastors is a great place to start. Maybe you won't stake your city. Fine, do whatever you have to do to focus on breaking the powers of hell over your city.

DON'T NEGLECT THE PROMISES ALREADY GIVEN

Prayer intercession is recognizing and standing against territorial spirits that lie behind the chronic historical problems in our cities. Through intercessory prayer, we can release the power of revival into every part of our cities with measured results seen in salvations and deliverance. Maybe you have received promises, visions, dreams or prophetic words for your city. Dig them out and begin to intercede over them. We at City Bible Church have used several different visions and city prophecies for the church of Portland as a source of prayer intercession for our city. The following is a sampling of what we have used:

JOHN G. LAKE:

> To my amazement, on approaching the building, high in the atmosphere, half a mile or more, I discerned millions of demons, organized as a modern army. There were those who apparently acted as shock troops. They would charge with great ferocity, followed by a wave, and yet another wave, and yet another wave. After a little while, I observed there operated a restraining influence that constituted a barrier through which they could not force themselves. With all the ingenuity of humans at war, this

multitude of demons seemed to endeavor to break the barrier or to go further, but were utterly restrained.... "Teach the people to pray for this. For this, and this alone, will meet the necessity of the human heart, and this alone will have the power to overcome the forces of darkness." As the angel was departing he said, "Pray. Pray. Pray. Teach the people to pray. Prayer and prayer alone, much prayer. Persistent prayer is the door of entrance into the heart of God."[8]

FRANK DAMAZIO:

If you had ears to hear in the spirit realm, you would hear thousands and millions of voices. The voices that are crying out are the voices of evil, voices of evil saying, "Give us this city! Give us the souls of these people!" If you had ears to hear, you would hear the words of the darkness crying out, "Give us this city! Give us this region!" They are pressing into the heavenlies, but they come up against an invisible force that surrounds the city. "The force," saith the Lord, "is the force of the prayers that are going up around the city." And as the demons press in, they can't press through, and they cry out to one another, "Where can we go to press in? Where can we go to find the way? Where can we go to make room? Where can we go to devastate?" But the angels cry back and forth, "There is no entry. There is no way. There is no path into our region." For the Lord has cried aloud through the people and through the saints of the Most High. "There is a covering," saith the Lord. "A covering," saith the Lord. "You're resisting. You're holding back the demonic forces. They cannot come through.

Do not let up. Do not pull back. This a day of victory, a day of hungering, a day of shattering the forces of evil," saith the Lord. "O press, press and press and press in," saith the Lord. "Press, press, for the evil forces are moving back. They are moving back. They are not penetrating," saith the Lord. "I will give you total and absolute victory in your cities if you would press. Do not smite the ground once or twice, but smite the ground over and over again," saith the Lord. "Smite it until the victory is complete. Press, press," saith the Lord.[9]

CINDY JACOBS:

A word for this city: "Have I not given you anointing to heal nations? And from this place I'm going to raise up a strong prayer tower, and I'm going to raise up the watch that will come from this city. And the anointing from this watch will be the anointing to break New Age. I'm going to bring forth an anointing from this city. I'm raising up intercessors; I'm raising up prophets. And the word of the Lord will come forth and the Lord says, 'I will tear down the idolatry to the occult. I will tear down the idolatry to humanism. And the word will go out in the Spirit that no longer will this be a haven for New Age,' says God, 'because I'm going to turn it around.... I'm getting ready to manifest myself as the God of glory in this city, I'm going to release a river of miracles; I'm going to release signs and wonders. I'm going to release creative miracles.... I am going to do a new thing. And I'm pouring out upon this generation, not just in one church, but upon the church of Portland and the surrounding areas. I'm going to cause My name to be glorified and people will come from the nations and they will come from far and wide to receive the impartation for the miraculous. I'm going to begin to impart the anointing for signs and wonders and miracles. You have come hungry and you have said, "Where is the God of Elijah?" I will pour out the Elisha anointing upon this generation of leaders. I will astound the wisdom of the wise. I'm going to release a mixture of miracles and will cause this city to be a city of refuge. I will cause this city to be raised up as a standard. I am raising up a standard, and from this place, I'm going to not only heal bodies, but I'm also going to heal this city. I'm going to heal the economy. I'm going to make this city a model that many people from governments—city governments from around the United States—will be flying in to see because I am causing a new anointing to come upon this city. They will marvel because I'm going to be glorified in city government. I'm going to be glorified in the health and human services. I'm going to be glorified in the social services. Look and see what I am going to do because I am going to reverse the order. I am going to put the government upon My shoulders and the lawgiver will go forth out of Zion. Watch and see for anything you dream is too small. Anything you believe I could do with this city is too small. In the next few months, you're even going to begin to see signs in the heavens. I am going to begin to do dramatic things to display My glory. I am going to start exporting this around the world. And you're going to go forth from this place with healing in your hands for I am going to arise with healing in My wings. I am going to heal the educational system. I am going to heal the legal system. I am going to transform this city. And I am going to use it for a model to America and the nations.'"[10]

Just five days after Cindy Jacobs gave this prophecy, a tremendous sign appeared in the heavens which was documented in *The Oregonian*:

> Only four meteorites have been found in Oregon. The last one hit a roof in Salem on May 13, 1981.
>
> A large, bright fireball flashed through the sky Sunday night, startling witnesses throughout the Portland area and the northern Willamette Valley.
>
> The spectacular fireball appeared shortly before 11 P.M. and lasted only a few seconds, emitting blue, green, yellow and orange flashes as it streaked east of Portland toward the southwest before shattering.
>
> "Fragments of the fast-moving fireball may have been able to survive the fiery plunge through the atmosphere," said Jim Todd, astronomy education coordinator for the Oregon Museum of Science and Industry. Todd said he received dozens of calls from witnesses.
>
> "This thing was huge and close," said Ray Beckwith, an architect who lives in Oregon City. "You actually could see the flames coming off the back of it. It was as big around as the moon and coming in at a fairly steep angle. I could see pieces breaking off of it. I believe there must be a piece of it out there somewhere."[11]

PRAYERWALKING

Securing borders also involves what Steve Hawthorne and Graham Kendrick termed "prayerwalking." Prayerwalking is simply walking while praying specific, directed, intentional prayers in a very unsuspecting and non-attention-drawing way. To see our neighborhoods and workplaces as they really are, we need to add a simple ingredient: prayerwalking.

This kind of praying is seeking to release God's blessing over the area, praying that His grace, mercy and redeeming love be released over the person or the place prayed for. Anyone and everyone can accomplish this type of on-site praying. Prayerwalking is not new; Scripture reveals numerous examples of this kind of prayer:

Arise, walk in the land through its length and its width, for I give it to you (Gen. 13:17).

Every place that the sole of your foot will tread upon I have given you, as I said to Moses (Josh. 1:3).

Then the men arose to go away; and Joshua charged those who went to survey the land, saying, "Go, walk through the land, survey it, and come back to me, that I may cast lots for you here before the LORD in Shiloh" (Josh. 18:8).

Prayerwalking is part of the believer's responsibility in discovering the fruit of the future, seeing our region filled with God's future blessings. As I have heard Ed Silvoso say on many occasions: "We must talk to God about our neighbor before we talk to our neighbors about God!" We need to prepare every place Jesus is about to go into. Scripture reveals the goal of prayerwalking—securing our borders:

After these things the Lord appointed seventy others also, and sent them two by two before His face *into every city and place* where He Himself was about to go. Then He said to them, "The harvest truly is great, but the laborers are few; therefore pray the Lord of the harvest to send out laborers into His harvest. Go your way; behold, I send you out as lambs among wolves" (Luke 10:1-3, italics added).

So Moses swore on that day, saying, "Surely the land where your foot has trodden shall be your inheritance and your children's forever, because you have wholly followed the LORD my God" (Josh. 14:9).

Prayerwalking is a practical way to secure the borders of our homes, neighborhoods and work places. Again, it may sound childish or foolish to the Western worldview because of its lack of any interest in the invisible realm, but for those of us who see prayerwalking, claiming, staking and anointing with oil as the tangible means for proclaiming spiritual truths, these simple actions do have powerful potential. As you read through the following verses, notice that God is very concerned with where, why and how we walk upon this earth:

You shall tread upon the lion and the cobra, the young lion and the serpent you shall trample underfoot (Ps. 91:13).

And the God of peace will crush Satan under your feet shortly. The grace of our Lord Jesus Christ be with you. Amen (Rom. 16:20).

To give light to those who sit in darkness and the shadow of death, to guide our feet into the way of peace (Luke 1:79).

And having shod your feet with the preparation of the gospel of peace (Eph. 6:15).

The purpose of prayerwalking is to further secure your spiritual borders, bless the people and the places, intercede, stand in the gap, bind principalities and powers, clear the air, and make way for the gospel to come in power. As you prayerwalk your neighborhood, you may face a difficult challenge represented in each home. Prayerwalking is moving the church into the community (see Acts 2:46,47).

Prayerwalking earth is our heavenly intercession; it allows the people of the church to become the people of the neighborhood and the people of the city. The Holy Spirit prompts spiri-

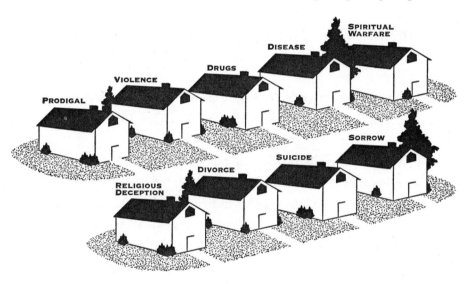

tual intercession with discernment that builds a perimeter of faith and secures our spiritual borders. As we practice this simple strategy for reaching our cities, we will encounter lost people and often these encounters will lead to conversions (see Ps. 2:8; Matt. 9:20-22).

When we begin to secure our borders with prayerwalking intercession, we will invade Satan's territory and we will discern the evil there with a heightened sensitivity to demonic and evil forces. We will enter into territories Satan has held for long periods of time with no intruders and no confrontations. We will become God's voice and instrument to bring down these powers and establish a beachhead for the power of the gospel to go forth. Getting righteous people out on the streets of our cities in a strategic, consistent manner may be one of the most effective means to reaching an entire city. The following Scriptures assure us that prayer can change the balance of spiritual power and make our cities more prepared to receive the power of Jesus.

> By the blessing of the upright the city is exalted, but it is overthrown by the mouth of the wicked (Prov. 11:11).

> For the weapons of our warfare are not carnal but mighty in God for pulling down strongholds (2 Cor. 10:4).

As we secure the borders of our neighborhoods, cities and states, we intercede for these places to be filled with the power of God that brings deliverance to individuals, health to families, restoration to marriages, gainful employment to the poor, wholesome recreational activities to the community, physical protection to both residents and businesses, spiritual peace to those who are confused, hunger for God to those who are apathetic toward Him, and restoration, refilling and revival in the Holy Spirit to our churches.

Pray that the territory within the perimeter of your city will be a place where the kingdom of God advances without hindrance and Satan's strongholds are destroyed. Pray that we will become the unified, covenant-keeping, intercessory-prayerwalking, faith-talking, life-transforming Church that we are called to be. We can secure our borders; we can reclaim our cities.

This Is Our City
By Mark Strauss

From the East (From the East),
To the West (To the West),
Let us all boldly confess:
"This is our city!"
"This is our city!"
From the North (From the North),
To the South (To the South),
Satan must give it up now.
"This is our city!"
"This is our city!"

Right here we stake our claim;
The whole city for Jesus' name.
We take back and now reclaim
Every border.

There's no demon authority
To stop us from victory.
So let's conquer this city,
Every border.[12]

PERSONAL APPLICATION

1. Prayerlessness is pridefulness; it says that we can do it without God's help. Is prayer a priority in your personal schedule? Have you made prayer a priority in your church or ministry?

2. Have you staked your neighborhood or your city to geographically proclaim repentance over the city? What corporate sins of the city do you and other leaders need

to repent for, forsake and publicly apologize for?

3. What are you doing to create unity in your city? Are you willing to meet with other leaders who do not agree with you on every issue? If so, make a list of those you will contact and agree to meet for breakfast.

4. Are you willing to become God's voice and instrument to bring down the demonic powers in your city and to establish a beachhead for the power of the gospel to go forth? Will you make a commitment to prayerwalking on a consistent basis?

Notes

1. George Otis, Jr., *Informed Intercession* (Ventura, CA: Regal Books, 1999), prepublished manuscript.
2. Saint Augustine, source unknown.
3. Frank Damazio, *Seasons of Intercession* (Portland, OR: City Bible Publishing, 1998).
4. Ed Silvoso, *That None Should Perish* (Ventura, CA: 1994), p. 23.
5. John Dawson, *Healing America's Wounds* (Ventura, CA: Regal Books, 1994), p. 47.
6. Ibid., p. 29.
7. Bob Beckett, *Commitment to Conquer* (Grand Rapids: Chosen Books, 1997), p. 128.
8. John G. Lake, *His Life and Sermons* (Fort Worth: Kenneth Copeland Publications, 1994), n. p.
9. Prophetic word given by Frank Damazio at the Winter Prayer Conference, January 18, 1997 during the evening service.
10. Cindy Jacobs, Northwest Summer Revival Conference, Portland, OR: July 22, 1997.
11. Richard L. Hill, "Fireball Streaks Across Oregon Sky," *The Oregonian*, 29 July 1997, B10.
12. Mark Strauss, "This Is Our City," City Bible Music, 1997. Used with permission.

CHAPTER 12

LOOSING CITIES FROM THE POWERS OF DARKNESS

The way of the wicked is like darkness; they do not know what makes them stumble.

PROVERBS 4:19

A member of our church had a vivid dream about hell and the powers of darkness; this dream was given to me in writing. It is as follows:

I saw hell as surrounded by a large iron fence. Christians were patrolling the fence and watching for those inside to come near the fence, being drawn by the light and sounds that came from outside. As those inside approached the fence, the Christians would reach through the bars, grab the lost and drag them through the fence into the kingdom of light. The only ones who were rescued were those who were drawn to the light, those who were free enough to be able to reach out and look for help.

Then I saw that as the Church was storming the gates of hell, the gates were knocked loose and hung open on their hinges. The Christians then marched through the gates and into the strongholds of hell. As they strode through the dark halls, they would stop at one cell after another and look at the prisoner inside. Each prisoner's body was bound tightly with one set of chains; another set chained the prisoner to the wall of the cell; the cell doors were also locked.

When a Christian looked inside, he would point to a cell and declare, "That one is destined for the kingdom of God. Release him." The chains would then break free from the walls and the cell door would open. The Christian would then go to another door and say, "That one is God's. Free him." And the cell door would fly open, as the chains knocked loose. The rescued ones were led out of the dark halls, through the courtyard of hell and into the kingdom of light.

This woman's vision could be an accurate description of the horrible bondage many people face in our cities. For so long we have been content to remain on the outskirts, rescuing those who manage to slip far enough away from the clutches of the enemy that they are lured to the light. But now it is time to march into the depths of hell and free those who are chained in darkness and bring them out. The covering of darkness over our cities is very real and powerful.

CITIES WITHOUT FORM AND VOID

Genesis 1:2 describes the earth before the moving of the Spirit of God. It may also depict our cities in desperate need of the creative power of the Holy Spirit:

The earth was without form, and void; and darkness was
on the face of the deep. And the Spirit of God was hovering over the face of the waters.

26 Translations of the Old Testament reads: "And the earth was
waste and void," "unformed and void," "invisible and unfurnished," "a formless wasteland," "chaotic," "had existed waste
and void," "a shapeless chaotic mass," and "darkness hung over
the deep," "and darkness was on the face of the roaring deep,"
"and while a mighty wind swept over the waters."[1]

If you substitute the word "city" for "earth" and read the verse
out loud, you may see a direct parallel with your city: a city that is
a wasteland, void, unfurnished, formless, chaotic—a shapeless
mass with darkness hung over it—its only hope is the hovering creative Spirit of God. Our cities are like the raging waves of a dark
sea, tossing, turning, throwing themselves against the darkness—
no escape, no hope, no future, unless the Spirit of God blows His
creative breath over those raging waters to bring new life.

The two negative Hebrew words used in this verse for "without form" and "void" are a double expression to describe the
utmost of an unformed, unshaped mass. These two Hebrew
words, *tohu* and *bohu,* denote that this confused mass had
remained this way, unchanged, for a long period of time.
"Without form" is the Hebrew word *tohu,* meaning to lie waste, a
desolation, desert land, a worthless thing, confusion, to have no
order, chaos, unformed. *Tohu* is translated in other Old
Testament verses to describe a desert wasteland (see Deut. 32:10;
Job 6:18), a destroyed city (see Isa. 24:10), a moral and spiritual
emptiness with confusion (see 1 Sam. 12:21; Isa. 29:21, 44:9;
45:19), and a nothingness and unreality (see Isa. 49:4).[2] All of
these descriptions accurately describe the state of the cities we
strategize to reach. The challenge is staggering—through human

eyes hopeless, intimidating and impossible. Why even start? Because our hope is in the Word of God and the supernatural power of the Holy Spirit.

HOSHEK DARKNESS

The Hebrew word for "darkness" in Genesis 1:2 is *hoshek* which means a covering of darkness, a covering that influences everything it touches.[3] In Exodus 10:21,22 *hoshek* refers to a darkness that can be felt, a thick darkness that covered the land:

> Then the Lord said to Moses, "Stretch out your hand toward heaven, that there may be darkness over the land of Egypt, darkness which may even be felt." So Moses stretched out his hand toward heaven, and there was thick darkness in all the land of Egypt three days.

Hoshek is a darkness that covers people's lives, influencing every part of their lives until they ultimately "sit down" under the covering of darkness:

> Those who sat in darkness and in the shadow of death, bound in affliction and irons (Ps. 107:10).

> They do not know, nor do they understand; they walk about in darkness; all the foundations of the earth are unstable (Ps. 82:5).

Hoshek is a darkness that darkens people's understanding. Their lives are filled with darkness; they sit in darkness, and they walk in darkness. Darkness brings calamity, ignorance, gloom, anguish and oppression. Darkness has the power to drive people into more and more darkness until everything about their lives is flooded in darkness:

> Then they will look to the earth, and see trouble and darkness, gloom of anguish; and they will be driven into darkness (Isa. 8:22).

> I sink in deep mire, where there is no standing; I have come into deep waters, where the floods overflow me (Ps. 69:2).

Our cities are covered with *hoshek* darkness, and the people are servants to this thick, felt, driving force. The hope we have is a Genesis 1:2 hope: "And the Spirit of God was hovering over the face of the waters." As we learn the power of prayer intercession coupled with repentance and brokenness, we can believe the

City reaching involves darkness piercing and removing the covering of darkness from our cities so that the light of the gospel can be received.

hovering Spirit of God for a mighty wind to sweep over our cities, forcing the state of nothingness and emptiness to surrender to the fullness of God. This does not happen, however, in one instantaneous act, but through a persistent, continuous Holy Spirit process.

Our cities do have a *hoshek* darkness, but they are ripe to receive a *ruah* (Hebrew: spirit, breath) of God to penetrate that darkness. City reaching involves darkness piercing and removing the covering of darkness from our cities so that the light of the gospel can be received. Genesis 1:4 says, "And God saw the light, that it was good; and God divided the light from the darkness." God desires to divide the darkness in our cities.

SKOTTA DARKNESS

In Greek, the word for darkness is *skotta*, *skotos* or *stokeinos* which means to be full of darkness or completely covered with darkness. This Greek word is translated "dark" in Luke 11:36 and "full of darkness" in Matthew 6:23 and Luke 11:34 where the physical condition is figurative of the moral. The group of *skot* words is derived from a root *ska* meaning to cover.[4] (See John 1:5; 8:12; 12:35,46; Rom. 2:19; 1 John 1:5; 2:8,9,11.) This *skotta* darkness denotes a spiritual or moral darkness emblematic of sin as a condition of moral or spiritual depravity. It is a darkness that covers the city, covers the people and affects every area of life:

- Darkness affects comprehension.
  And the light shines in the darkness, and the darkness did not comprehend it (John 1:5).

- Darkness affects lifestyle.
  Then Jesus spoke to them again, saying, "I am the light of the world. He who follows Me shall not walk in darkness, but have the light of life" (John 8:12).

- Darkness can overtake people.
  Then Jesus said to them, "A little while longer the light

is with you. Walk while you have the light, lest darkness overtake you; he who walks in darkness does not know where he is going" (John 12:35).

- Darkness can be broken.
I have come as a light into the world, that whoever believes in Me should not abide in darkness (John 12:46).

This is the message which we have heard from Him and declare to you, that God is light and in Him is no darkness at all (1 John 1:5).

- Darkness will pass away.
Again, a new commandment I write to you, which thing is true in Him and in you, because the darkness is passing away, and the true light is already shining. He who says he is in the light, and hates his brother, is in darkness until now (1 John 2:8,9).

- Darkness is strengthened through hatred.
But he who hates his brother is in darkness and walks in darkness, and does not know where he is going, because the darkness has blinded his eyes (1 John 2:11).

And are confident that you yourself are a guide to the blind, a light to those who are in darkness (Rom. 2:19).

- Darkness can dominate cities through evil spiritual powers.
For we do not wrestle against flesh and blood, but against principalities, against powers, against the rulers of the darkness of this age, against spiritual hosts of wickedness in the heavenly places. Therefore take up the whole armor

of God, that you may be able to withstand in the evil day, and having done all, to stand (Eph. 6:12,13).

Then the fifth angel poured out his bowl on the throne of the beast, and his kingdom became full of darkness; and they gnawed their tongues because of the pain (Rev. 16:10).

- Darkness torments people through evil spirits.
But the Spirit of the LORD departed from Saul, and a distressing spirit from the Lord troubled him (1 Sam. 16:14).

And when the unclean spirit had convulsed him and cried out with a loud voice, he came out of him (Mark 1:26).

And always, night and day, he was in the mountains and in the tombs, crying out and cutting himself with stones (Mark 5:5).

A DARKNESS THAT CAN BE FELT

Whole cities, regions, states and nations can be dominated by a thick covering of darkness. "A darkness that can be felt" is a correct biblical description of darkness that persists over many and most cities:

Now when Jesus heard that John had been put in prison, He departed to Galilee. And leaving Nazareth, He came and dwelt in Capernaum, which is by the sea, in the regions of Zebulun and Naphtali, that it might be fulfilled which was spoken by Isaiah the prophet, saying: "The land of Zebulun and the land of Naphtali, by the way of the sea, beyond the Jordan, Galilee of the Gentiles: The people who sat in darkness have seen a great light, and upon those who sat in the region and shadow of death light has dawned. From that time Jesus began to preach and to say, 'Repent, for the kingdom of heaven is at hand'" (Matt. 4:12-17).

Notice that the darkness affected the people to the point that they sat in darkness, resting, enjoying the darkness. The darkness was upon a region, a geographical darkness, in the land of Zebulun and Naphtali. A seat of Satan is a geographic location that is highly oppressed and demonically controlled by a certain

An increased exposure to immorality and

vulgarity desensitizes people and leads to a

diminished ability to discern good from evil.

dark principality. From this demonic seat the enemy conducts warfare on the city, region, state or nation.[5] To penetrate the regions of darkness, we must discern where the seats of Satan exist and how to successfully destroy them spiritually. We must discern our Zebulun and Naphtali.

EACH REGION IS UNIQUE IN DARKNESS

Each region has its unique historical, cultural differences and spiritual destiny (see Matt. 4:15,16; Acts 17:5,9; 18:9,10).

Each region has its own unique level of darkness (see Exod. 10:21; Isa. 60:2). When you compare the levels of darkness in certain cities to others, it is very obvious that some have thick, deep, felt, controlling darkness while others have weak darkness, easily penetrated. Every region must be spiritually discerned and then strategized.

Each region has people darkness unique at that time to that region. In 1980 a news broadcaster presented a segment about residents living in the Loveland area of New York State who exhibited an unusually high frequency of cancer and leukemia. An investigative search revealed a toxic waste leakage that flowed into the residential water tables, infecting hundreds of families. These unsuspecting people were living right on top of life-threatening chemicals, but were unaware that these unseen toxins were slowly seeping into their bodies. Darkness upon a region will have a deep impact upon the people who sit under it for years, decades and generations. Violence, immorality, occult and many other forms of spiritism, witchcraft and New Age will seep into the water tables and slowly destroy every area of spiritual and domestic life (see Ps. 143:3; Prov. 2:13; 4:19; Isa. 42:7; John 3:19).

DESENSITIZED BY DARKNESS

The spiritual covering of darkness over a region will slowly transform the people of that region. When a city culture is given over to evil powers and evil practices, the door for demonization is opened and people may be influenced by or ignorantly welcoming evil spirits into their lives. Luke 22:3 states that Satan entered into Judas Iscariot, and Acts 5:3 states that Satan filled the heart of Ananias, causing him to lie to the Holy Spirit and to withhold part of the money he and his wife Sapphira made when they sold a piece of property. In both cases, evil had profound influence upon the human heart, mind, will and emotions.

People who live under a thick covering of darkness may well be candidates for Satan to fill their lives with his power to do evil. Today's culture sits under individualism and secularism, and relativistic values envelope people and condition their minds and spirits. An increased exposure to immorality and vulgarity desensitizes people and leads to a diminished ability to discern good from evil.

This world's darkness of covetousness, ambition, lust, intellectual pride, sensuality, materialism and worldly prestige makes for a darkness that can be felt and a darkness that must be penetrated. The apostle Paul described this doctrine of darkness as this present evil age (see Gal. 1:4), the prince of the power of the air (see Eph. 2:2) and those who walk according to this world (see Col. 1:13).

DARKNESS VERSUS LIGHT

This present evil age of darkness is contrasted to the age of light and righteousness in which Christ reigns above all evil rule, authority and power of dominion. These two powers, darkness and light, stand in direct opposition with strong conflict. One is a kingdom of sin and death in which demonic powers seek to influence, rule and torment people's lives. The other is the kingdom of life and righteousness in which Christ is Lord, bringing freedom and destiny to people's lives.

Paul states in 2 Corinthians 5:17, "Therefore, if anyone is in Christ, he is a new creation; old things have passed away; behold, all things have become new" and in Colossians 1:13, "He has delivered us from the power of darkness and conveyed us into the kingdom of the Son of His love." (Also see Eph. 1:20,21.)

God has given us the power to penetrate this darkness over people's lives and the geographically dark areas where they live. Our mandate is "to open their eyes, in order to turn them from darkness to light, and from the power of Satan to God, that they may receive forgiveness of sins and an inheritance among those who are sanctified by faith in Me" (Acts 26:18).

DISMANTLING THE DARKNESS WITH SPIRITUAL EQUIPMENT

We, as the City Church, need the following spiritual equipment to successfully deal with the spiritual darkness over people, places, cities and regions:

- We need spiritual perception and spiritual intelligence to see things undetected by natural eyes. We need spiritual discernment about people and geographical areas and insight to judge whether the source behind the power is human, satanic or Holy Spirit generated.
- We need a biblical worldview which understands that there is both a spiritual realm and a material realm. Behind the visible is the invisible. Demonic forces may be very active in our Western society and yet totally undetected by the Western worldview. Though many Westerners retain a vague belief in God, most deny that other supernatural beings even exist. Indeed, unlike most of the peoples of the world, we Westerners divide the world into what we call the natural and the supernatural; then we largely disregard the supernatural. The Westerner's skepticism and scientific rationalism says that if something cannot be seen, measured or proven through reason, it simply

does not exist or, at the very least, should be doubted (see Acts 6:12,13).

- We need to establish strategic prayer centers in every city, in every church and then in every Holy Spirit covered home that will open up a gate to heaven to break through the thick covering of evil and darkness (see Gen. 28:15-17; John 1:5; 8:12). We must recognize and stand against the territorial spirits that lie behind the chronic historical problems in our cities. We do this through intercessory prayer, preaching the cross of Christ, and moving in the supernatural with power to deliver people (see John 8:12).

- We need to believe in the power of the gospel to penetrate darkness in any and all cities, delivering people and places from evil influences. We need to believe that we, the City Church, can reach every person and bring every household in touch with the true power and love of a living God. We need to release the whole church to reach the whole city with the whole gospel (see Rom. 2:19; Col. 1:13).

PAVING A POWER PATH

For it is the God who commanded light to shine out of darkness, who has shone in our hearts to give the light of the knowledge of the glory of God in the face of Jesus Christ (2 Cor. 4:6).

But you are a chosen generation, a royal priesthood, a holy nation, His own special people, that you may proclaim the praises of Him who called you out of darkness into His marvelous light (1 Pet. 2:9).

The City Church will become the people of power. Everywhere we go, a power path will open up as we become humble servants dependent upon God to release His power through us. The New Testament clearly indicates that the power of God is meant to accompany the gospel and to find expression through the lives of those to whom and through whom the message comes. It is right to bring the supernatural into prominence and to raise Christians' expectations with regard to it. It is right to want to be a channel of divine power into people's lives at their point of need.

As a City Church, we must desire to see the evil chains of darkness broken off any and all people who come in contact with the power of God. Chains broken off:

- Those who are economically and morally poor.
- Those who have spiritually become captives of demonic powers, oppressed of the devil; those with physical infirmities.
- Those who are blinded spiritually by the god of this world.
- Those who are captives of witchcraft, any form of the occult, or any kind of religious deception.
- Those who are under a curse: from the ignorant or intentional use of witchcraft, other hoaxes or games, demonic curses or people curses. Those who have become increasingly disoriented or confused, continuously emotionally drained or debilitated, or increasingly plagued by inordinate fears.

Come, let us pierce the darkness, let us declare war on the city strongholds!

Arise, shine; for your light has come! And the glory of the LORD is risen upon you. For behold, the darkness shall cover the earth, and deep darkness the people; but the LORD will arise over you, and His glory will be seen upon you. The Gentiles shall come to your light, and kings to the brightness of your rising (Isa. 60:1-3).

CHANGING THE ATMOSPHERE

The city can become a place where the spiritual atmosphere changes dramatically, allowing a new surge of Holy Spirit activity. Atmosphere speaks of a pervading or surrounding influence or spirit, a general mood or environment. In 2 Chronicles 5:13,14, the atmosphere of the Temple was changed by the prayer and unity of the priests, and "the house of the LORD, was filled with a cloud."

In Genesis 28:10-17, Jacob experienced an atmosphere change when God showed up. Jacob's response was "How awesome is this place! This is none other than the house of God, and this is the gate of heaven!" Our cities can be a gateway to the supernatural, a place where God abides and His power is actively released.

TWELVE ATMOSPHERE GOALS

The following are 12 atmosphere goals to pursue:

1. An atmosphere of **Open Heavens**: No spiritual hindrances allowed—breakthrough.

   We all have seasons when we are pressed on every side, darkness abounds, and the heavens seem as brass. The same thing can happen to a church or city. And, as in the case of most individuals, churches and cities can also achieve breakthrough. The forces of darkness can be pushed back through prayer, worship, unity and servanthood. Strongholds of poverty, sickness, crime and violence can all be broken. And God can open the windows of Heaven and pour out hope, healing and revival. In the book of Luke, Jesus sent disciples ahead of Him into every town. They healed the sick, announced the kingdom of God and rebuked demons. Satan fell like lightening. They had open heavens. We can experience the same thing today. Let's open the heavens in our churches and cities to prepare for Jesus.

2. An atmosphere of **Unified Expectancy:** No "business as usual" services.

If you announced that Jesus was going to appear in bodily form at your next service, the atmosphere around your church would be a lot different. People would arrive early, ball games would be taped (or forgotten altogether), and lost loved ones would be physically dragged through the doors. No one would stay home because they felt under the weather. In fact, the prospect of a healing touch from Jesus would be added incentive to race to church. And yet, Jesus has already promised to be in our midst every time we come together. Let's live like it! Remember, He did very few miracles in His hometown (see Matt. 13:58). God help us if we're guilty of a "hometown" attitude. Jesus Christ is the most exciting, inspiring and power-filled personality in the universe. When He shows up, no one sleeps in the pews. Give the Holy Spirit some liberty during your next service; then get excited—Jesus is in the house!

3. An atmosphere of **Supernatural Surprises**: He's no common, ordinary God we serve.

Jesus' first miracle was that of creating 150 gallons of very fine wine. This was no ordinary wedding gift, and He's no ordinary God. He healed a centurion's servant whom He had never met, yet let a dear friend, Lazarus, rot in a tomb for four days before raising him. He rebuked religious leaders and violently threw people out of church, but forgave adulteresses. He even stored his tax payment in a fish's mouth. God is awesomely supernatural, but He's not ordinary. Who could guess...that a struggling church in Toronto, Ontario, would touch churches worldwide through renewal? That a simple drama called "Eternity" would lead more than 30,000 people to salvation during its first 12 months? That pastors would come together to pound stakes into the ground and see crime rates plummet in their city? God has supernatural surprises in store for your church and your city—supernatural power that will heal, deliver, revive and restore. Just realize that the way God releases His supernatural power will probably surprise you.

4. An atmosphere of **Everyone Can Receive**: No limitations allowed to be placed on anyone.

Rahab was a prostitute, yet she's included as a champion of faith in Hebrews 11. Paul was vicious in his persecution of the Church, but he brought the gospel to the Gentiles. David committed murder and adultery; Mary Magdalene was filled with demons; Gideon was a coward.

There is no limit to what God can do with a life. Jesus promised to give the Holy Spirit to everyone who asks—Holy Spirit power, faith, healing, vision, peace, boldness, energy and life. There is no room for condemnation and unbelief in the kingdom of God, especially right now. If God puts no limitations on a person's life, neither should we.

5. An atmosphere of **People Are Important:** No person is undervalued here.

Flowers come in all shapes and sizes, some soft and delicate, others strong and thorny, yet each one has a unique fragrance and beauty. People are God's garden; they are His bouquet, and He loves variety. In fact, Revelation says that He's purchased them from every tribe, language, people and nation (see Rev. 5:9). People are our inheritance and valuing them is what the gospel is all about. No, there's not many wise, not many mighty, and very few noble. In fact, they come just like the rest of us—thorny, fragile, and in desperate need of sun, rain and pruning. We just need to love and to recognize how beautiful each one becomes in the hands of the Master Gardener.

6. An atmosphere of **Victorious Living Is Possible:** No defeatist spirit; God is able to deliver anyone at anytime.

We've all quoted the verses, "If God is for us, who can be against us?" (Rom. 8:31); "I can do all things through Christ"(Phil. 4:13), and Nothing, absolutely nothing, is impossible with God (see Matt. 19:26). But we are entering a season in which the Church needs to be charged with the power of these truths so that fear doesn't stand a chance. We can look adversity in the eye and know that God is powerfully working every detail to our advantage. It's genuine faith. Confidence in a God who is for us....Who spared not His own Son and will graciously give us all things. It's a lifestyle that's contagious. It gives hope to the hopeless, makes a way when there is no way, causes darkness to flee in terror, and releases the miraculous power of a God who knows no defeat.

7. An atmosphere of **Reaching Our City:** No "hold the fort" philosophy here; we attack and take no prisoners.

There are times of visitation for every city. Jerusalem missed one of its times, causing Jesus to weep. Nineveh responded and received mercy and revival. There is also a time of visitation for our cities. God is zealous to break every demonic stronghold—pornography, crime, prejudice, poverty, New Age—and to release compassion and life. There is an anointing on the Church to reach cities. Denominational barriers are crumbling, prayer is on the rise, young people are touching their generation, and darkness is running for cover. Joshua and Caleb looked beyond the giants to a land flowing with milk and honey. Our cities are no more challenging than those Joshua and Caleb faced. Spiritual Amorites and Canaanites will flee before us as grasshoppers. God longs to touch our cities, and we're His partners. Just like Joshua and Caleb, we are well able to take the land.

8. An atmosphere of **Financial Blessing**: No excuses or apologies; God is good and He desires to bless and provide for His work.

Abraham, Joseph, David, Solomon and Job—these were some of the earth's wealthiest people. Each one received his wealth from God. God is not afraid of riches. In fact, He is rich in every regard and the source of all true riches. Why then do we shy from riches? We're commanded to care for the poor, send missionaries, preach the gospel to the ends of the earth, and reach our cities for Christ. It all takes money—lots of it. God is good. He desires above all things that we prosper and be in health as our soul prospers (see 3 John 1:2). God is a giver and finds great delight in blessing His children. Let's receive it gratefully and then follow His example. The Bible says, "Give and it shall be given," "The generous soul will prosper," and "He that gives to the poor lends to the Lord." This year take liberality to a new level and then receive the promised blessing.

9. An atmosphere of **Communion**: Where the voice of God is heard clearly.

His voice, though seldom discernible to the natural ear, is the most powerful sound there is. One word from Him and the most troubled heart is comforted, the most confused circumstances are made clear, and the most fragmented relationships are healed. These are exhilarating days for the Church. We are seeing a fresh outpouring of the Spirit, growing churches, an increase of the miraculous, power encounters and healings. But what is affecting the lives of people the most is hearing Him. God is talking to His people. He is revealing His love one word at a time. Decade-long bondages are broken in a moment. Prayer is taking on an added dimension: listening. More can be said in silence than from the pulpit, because it is Jesus who is speaking. Remember the story of Mary and Martha? Martha busily set the table and prepared the meal. Mary seemingly ignored her responsibilities and sat idly with Jesus. Yet Jesus said Mary chose the better part (see Luke 10:42). In our Western culture, where activity is king and where success is measured by the entries in the daytimer, let's not neglect the better part. Let's keep our ears ever tuned to His voice.

10. An atmosphere of **Faith:** No pessimism about the future; God is in control.

Books about the end of the age have been topping bestseller lists for years. Deadlines pass and new books are written. As I write this, the prophets of Y2K are dominating the headlines. They seem to forget that God is in control and that not even a sparrow falls to the ground without His knowledge. God is our Father. He has promised to feed and clothe us and to fulfill every word that proceeds from His mouth. We serve a good God and the future is in His hands. He's promised a glorious Church without spot or wrinkle. We're not there yet, but we will be. How about your life? Are there still promises to be fulfilled? Then go for them; God is with you. Doesn't He want our loved ones saved, our cities transformed, and the gospel preached to every nation? Absolutely! And He's not going to leave His work undone.

11. An atmosphere of **Vision:** Where people see the invisible and do the impossible.

What do you see when you look at your church? Is it filled with worldly teenagers, uncommitted fathers, budget shortfalls and carpet that needs replacing? Or do you see as God sees...tear-filled altars, discarded crutches, healed families, ethnic diversity and the shout of triumph. He sees lifelong bondages to alcohol, drugs or pornography shattered, bitterness washed away in forgiveness, and families restored. He sees our cities' red-light districts overrun with churches, the poor being fed, the prisons emptied and Bibles in classrooms. God sees things the way they can be. He sees with the eyes of faith. We must do the same. Only then can we do the things God sees us doing.

12. An atmosphere of **Worship:** Where the river of God is released in fullness.

True worship comes from the heart. It can happen in the quietness of our personal devotions or while cruising on a six-lane interstate highway, but there is a dynamic that's released in corporate worship when musicians and voices abandon themselves totally to adore the Savior. It's called the river of God. It's a tangible sense of the Holy Spirit's presence where faith arises, hearts are refreshed, and the circumstances of our personal lives take on a new perspective. The river of God also impacts the heavenly realm. As God is enthroned on our praises, heaven rejoices, darkness is dispelled and His kingdom rule is extended. Lord, let every area of our personal lives and corporate services be marked by the spirit of worship. We grant You permission to interrupt our programs and discard our agendas to release worship. And Lord, let Your river flow.

When these 12 atmosphere changes are in place, our cities will be loosed, the shackles of bondage will be broken and the rescued ones will be led out of the dark corridors of hell and into the kingdom of light.

Pray
By Debbie Trujillo

Pray 'til the mountain moves.
Pray 'til the chains are loosed.
Pray 'til I raise up an army
From the valley of dry bones.

Pray through the darkest night.
Pray 'til you reach the prize.
Pray 'til I raise up an army
From the valley of dry bones.

"It's not by might.
It's not by power,
But by My Spirit," says the Lord.
"It's not by might.
It's not by power,
But by My Spirit," says the Lord.

Will you cry for the one who has no voice
'Til the power of Satan has been destroyed?
Stand in the gap for the one who is lost;
Lay down your life, not counting the cost.[6]

PERSONAL APPLICATION

1. Even Christians can become desensitized to the effects of evil around them. Take a moment to evaluate the felt darkness in your city. Rather than looking at the city, ask the Lord for eyes to see *into* the soul of your city. What steps will you take to confront the darkness in your city?

2. Before we can penetrate the darkness in the city, we must allow the searchlight of the Holy Spirit to reveal areas of darkness in our own lives. Has covetousness, ambition, lust, intellectual pride, sensuality, materialism or worldly prestige gripped you or desensitized you to the pain of others? If so, ask God to change your heart.

3. As you read through the 12 atmosphere goals, which ones do you most need to implement? Goals can only be achieved when those setting them make a commitment to take action. Will you list some steps you will take to change the atmosphere in your church?

Notes
1. *26 Translations of the Old Testament*, Genesis to Esther (Grand Rapids: Zondervan, 1985), p. 1.
2. Frank E. Gaebelein, *Expositor's Bible Commentary, New International Version, Vol. 2* (Grand Rapids: Zondervan, 1992), pp. 24, 25.

3. William Wilson, *Old Testament Word Studies* (Grand Rapids: Kregel Publications, 1978), p. 108.

4. W. E. Vine, *Vine's Expository Dictionary of New Testament Words* (Old Tappan, N. J.: Fleming H. Revell, 1966), p. 267.

5. C. Peter Wagner, *Breaking Strongholds* (Ventura, CA: Regal Books, 1993), p. 89.

6. Debbie Trujillo, "Pray," City Bible Music, 1997. Used with permission.

CHAPTER 13

A
VISION FOR
YOUR CITY

*Thus says the Lord GOD: "On the day that I cleanse
you from all your iniquities, I will also enable you to
dwell in the cities, and the ruins shall be rebuilt."*

EZEKIEL 36:33

My relationship with my city is in many ways like the relationship
I have with my wife; it's constantly growing. I loved her when we
got married, but the more I know about her hidden personality,
her unique giftings and her stalwart character, the more I love
her. My love grows as our relationship grows and we experience
more of life together: home, children, sorrow, pain, joy, disappointment, challenges and surprises.

When a pastor is called to a city the bonding process is
uniquely parallel to a romance, a marriage, a deepening relationship—a trying relationship! You may have experienced love
at first sight for your city, or it may have been less than love, even

disdain or disgust. Maybe you were trapped, snared, captured by circumstances: a word from God, a family situation or just going there for a little while and then moving on. A pastor's love for his city has a great deal to do with city reaching and city ministry.

The Marriage Between Church Call and City Call

If you were asked outright, "Do you love your church?" the answer most likely would be yes—but of course not without pain, sorrow, disappointment, glory days and gory days—but your love is real. The love for your city must be just as real and just as enduring. All cities have weaknesses and strengths, the reasons people love it and hate it there: the weather, traffic, population size, atmosphere, smell, ethnic mix or educational limitations. All or any of these factors could be the reason you love or tolerate your city.

If God has called you to your church, He has called you to your city. Our vision begins not only with our church's future, but also with our city's future. When you read the newspaper or listen to the news, do you find yourself listening with no interest, no real feelings about the problems: the murders, rapes, burglaries, drownings, bankruptcies or laws passed that are blatantly against God's Word? Does your heart response sound like this: *Whatever! The world is certainly messed up. I can't believe our politicians. There is no respect for God in our city! Well, let's see, what should I preach on Sunday? Ah, now this is more like it, preaching to the church.*

This complacent response is exactly why many of us who are spiritual leaders need a revival in our souls concerning our love and pastoral concern for our cities. God loves the people in your church and in your city. God desires to disciple cities, shape cities and pastor the people in our cities. We pastors and spiritual leaders have not been taught to love our cities as much as we love our churches.

LOVING YOUR CITY WHILE LOVING YOUR CHURCH

Permit me to share a little personal history here. My journey as a Christian leader seeking to be equipped for the ministry took me through Bible college, three seminaries, numerous conferences, seminars and other modes of education. I have a bachelor of theology, a master of divinity from Oral Roberts University, and

Why is evangelism so difficult in our twenty-first-century Church? Because we are not in the city and the city is not in us.

have done doctoral studies at Fuller Seminary and ORU. In all my hundreds of hours of classes, there was not one full-credit class on the relationship between the city and the pastor—how to love the city, pastor in the city, network in the city, be involved with city life, meet the social needs of the city, minister to the youth of the city, et cetera.

Most books offer ample material for the pastor and the church on the pastoral ministry and yet never mention the pastor and the city, let alone how to reach the city. We have been somewhat trained in preaching, teaching, counseling, prayer, administration, how to study, how to speak and how to run programs. But what happens to the city? Books abound on the subjects of ethical conduct, the pastor's wife, Sunday morning worship, midweek prayer meetings, evangelistic meetings, altar calls, dedications of infants, wedding ceremonies, funerals, ordination, finances, building programs and praying for the sick. But what happened to the city?

Is there really any question as to why most leaders and most churches are consumed with their own churches, having little or no contact with the outside world? Why is evangelism so difficult in our twenty-first-century Church? Because we are not in the city and the city is not in us. We have removed the candlestick from the city, removed the light, the oil, the ministry of Christ in and to the city. Our first calling is not to the one congregation we preach to, but to the whole city God has placed us in.

In Luke 10:1, we read that Jesus appointed 70 leaders to go two by two into every city and place where He Himself was about to go. God has appointed you and sent you into your city because God is coming to your city. He sent you to prepare a way for His presence and power to be released in your city. Jesus' heart for the city is revealed in Luke 19:41. Jesus is still outside of Jerusalem as He utters His lament, which only Dr. Luke records, a leader with deep feelings for his city:

> Now as He drew near, He saw the city and wept over it, saying, "If you had known, even you, especially in this your day, the things that make for your peace! But now they are hidden from your eyes. For days will come upon you when your enemies will build an embankment around you, surround you and close you in on every side, and level you, and your children within you, to the ground; and they will

not leave in you one stone upon another, because you did not know the time of your visitation" (Luke 19:41-44).

EVERY CITY HAS SPIRITUAL SEASONS

Jesus was the answer Jerusalem was seeking, but Jerusalem didn't know that. Jesus was the peace this city of tension and heartache needed, but had failed to find. The very name Jerusalem meant city of peace. Its day of visitation had come but the people could not recognize it. Jesus saw beyond the day; He saw the devastation coming—the future of the city—and He wept.

As leaders sent to our cities, we must be aware that there are prophetic moments, turning points, in our cities. When the turning point is missed, the future of the city is at stake. Jesus was the prophet who could foresee and the priest intercessor who could intercede. His heart was burdened and His vision for the city would not diminish even though the future would be devastating. Every city has a future, a destiny, a hope. We are to weep with God over our city's future.

Jesus speaks emphatically about the promised visitation for the city of Jerusalem in Luke 19:44: "because you did not know the time of your visitation." The time of visitation is set by God, but must be discerned by the city leadership. The visitation would come to an indifferent city and in their indifference the people would miss the time. Their obstinate resistance to Jesus would ultimately bring the city to ruin and overthrow the entire nation. The contrast between what was and what might have been was so great that Jesus could not refrain Himself from lamentation. He wept over His city. God will visit our cities either in revival and redemptive restoration or in judgment.

Our hope is that God would come to our cities to bless, to restore and to deliver (see Gen. 21:1; 1 Sam. 2:21). Failure to

know the time of visitation is followed by definite grave consequences—a spiritual deadness that cannot be remedied without
a shaking, a judgment or a time of spiritual barrenness.

SEASONS OF SOWING AND REAPING

As a spiritual leader in my cities (we reach two cities, Portland,
Oregon, and Vancouver, Washington, because they are geographically set together), I must have a heart and a vision for the visitation
of God to the city. I believe the cities of today have a tremendous
receptivity to the true gospel; our cities are full of opportunity.
Cities, like individuals and nations, are subject to seasons, specific
times to sow seed and specific times to reap the harvest.

What is the spiritual climate, the spiritual season of your city?
Ted Haggard refers to the spiritual climate as knowing the water
level of your city: "In the same way that water levels in a reservoir
change according to the time of year or amount of rainfall, so cities
and regions experience varying levels of the Holy Spirit's activity."[1]

I call this Holy Spirit activity "sowing and reaping seasons." I
will reap where I have not sowed and sow where I cannot reap. It
doesn't matter. What really matters is that someone reaps and
reaps well at the right time. When you are pastoring for the city and
not just for the church, sowing and reaping takes on a whole new
perspective.

We claim Acts 18:10: "I have many people in this city."
Enough people to overflow hundreds of churches by 10 times
their present church size. Let us not be concerned about our own
church growth but with the overall growth of the City Church.
Jesus had compassion for the multitudes. City reaching is the
ability to see all the people in the city in search of the living God.
The multitudes are there, but can we see them? I must embrace
the simple fact that if we are to reach a city, it will take the whole
City Church to reach the whole city.

A Nehemiah Attitude

Each individual spiritual leader in the city must nurture a Nehemiah attitude—a passionate and persevering heart to reach our cities for God. Jerusalem was a thousand miles away from Nehemiah's world. To journey from his world, his lifestyle and his job security through dangerous country with hostile enemies and robbers required quite a commitment from Nehemiah. Why would a man leave his comfort zone for a burned out, broken down, devastated city? The answer is that he loved his city! To leave your palace and move to a city that offers nothing but work, warfare and weakness, you must have a vision for that city.

The following diagram points out the men involved, books of the Bible and the time frame in which the project occurred:

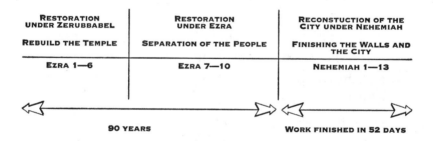

RESTORATION UNDER ZERUBBABEL	RESTORATION UNDER EZRA	RECONSTUCTION OF THE CITY UNDER NEHEMIAH
REBUILD THE TEMPLE	SEPARATION OF THE PEOPLE	FINISHING THE WALLS AND THE CITY
EZRA 1—6	EZRA 7—10	NEHEMIAH 1—13

90 YEARS   WORK FINISHED IN 52 DAYS

Nehemiah, as a city-reaching, city-restoring strategist, is a model for all leaders who have a vision for their cities. Nehemiah had a deep spiritual burden for the condition of his city and a vision to change it:

The words of Nehemiah the son of Hachaliah. It came to pass in the month of Chislev, in the twentieth year, as I was in Shushan the citadel, that Hanani one of my brethren came with men from Judah; and I asked them concerning the Jews who had escaped, who had survived the captivity, and concerning Jerusalem. And they said to me, "The survivors who are left from the captivity in the province are there in great distress and reproach. The wall of Jerusalem is also broken down, and its gates are burned with fire." So it was, when I heard these words, that I sat down and wept, and mourned for many days; I was fasting and praying before the God of heaven (Neh. 1:1-4).

Nehemiah's Prayer for the City

When Nehemiah heard the state of his city, his response was four months of fasting, praying, weeping and mourning. The biblical description of how the city was devastated by King Nebuchadnezzar is found in 2 Chronicles 36:18,19:

And all the articles from the house of God, great and small, the treasures of the house of the LORD, and the treasures of the king and of his leaders, all these he took to Babylon. Then they burned the house of God, broke down the wall of Jerusalem, burned all its palaces with fire, and destroyed all its precious possessions.

The magnificent place where God's glory was once displayed and respected by all nations was destroyed—the land in ruins, the city ruined, the temple destroyed and the people taken into Babylonian captivity:

And those who escaped from the sword he carried away to Babylon, where they became servants to him and his sons until the rule of the kingdom of Persia (2 Chron. 36:20).

This is an accurate description of our cities today around the world. Destroyed by moral perversity, diseases, corruption, violence, the worship of other gods, idolatry, occultism, pornography, abortion, euthanasia, child molestation, spousal abuse, discouragement, suicide, poverty, and addictions—our cities have been sacked by the kingdom of darkness.

In *Loving Your City into the Kingdom*, Jack Hayford speaks of his Holy Spirit encounter during prayer when he was shown that his city was being destroyed:

"You are not being told 'Los Angeles will be destroyed,' because this city is *already* being destroyed. It does not need a catastrophic disaster to experience destruction because the Destroyer is already at work. The toll you have recounted, which a severe earthquake might cost, is small in comparison to the reality that stalks this city every day.

More than mere thousands are being speared through by the shafts of hell's darts, seeking to take their souls. *More* than 150,000 homes (not merely houses) are being assailed by the sin and social pressures that rip families and marriages apart. *More* havoc is being wreaked by the invisible grindings of evil power than tectonic plates could ever generate. A liquefaction of the spiritual foundations that alone allow a society to stand is wiping out the underpinnings of relationships, of righteous behavior and of healthy lifestyle.

You are to pray against THIS—the present, ongoing, devastating destruction of the city of Los Angeles."[2]

But God is not going to allow these cities to continue under the principalities and powers of evil. God is raising up Nehemiahs who will leave the world of religious matters, job security, running church programs and running church committees to rebuild the city. God stirred up a heathen king named Cyrus, King of Persia, who overthrew Babylon to restore the city and rebuild the house of God. He released God's people to accomplish the vision:

> Now in the first year of Cyrus king of Persia, that the word of the LORD by the mouth of Jeremiah might be fulfilled, the LORD stirred up the spirit of Cyrus king of Persia, so that he made a proclamation throughout all his kingdom, and also put it in writing (2 Chron. 36:22).

Nehemiah was one of three key leaders to respond. First Zerubbabel, then Ezra and finally Nehemiah. Nehemiah was the king's cupbearer, a trusted prestigious position, before he became Nehemiah the city reacher and city rebuilder. Nehemiah's response to the challenge of reaching a city was prayer and fasting. Always, begin with prayer and fasting. Before we strategize, before we program, before we engage the enemy—pray!

Nehemiah prayed 11 important prayers:

• Intercessory prayer for God's house (Neh. 1:9-11)
• Prayer before the king (Neh. 2:4)
• Prayer to overcome discouragement (Neh. 4:4,5)
• Prayer for divine protection (Neh. 4:9)
• Prayer for personal needs (Neh. 5:19)
• Prayer for inner strength (Neh. 6:9)
• Prayer against opposition (Neh. 6:14)
• Prayer for the vision (Neh. 13:14)
• Prayer for spiritual leaders (Neh. 13:29)
• Prayer for the mercy of God (Neh. 13:22)
• Prayer for God's blessing (Neh. 13:31)

Nehemiah's vision for the city aroused in him a desire to ask the Lord to send him to meet the need (see Neh. 2:15; Isa. 49:10,11). He was motivated to go and spy out the land first-hand (see Neh. 2:13-18) and then to strategize. Nehemiah was tested, attacked, accused and faced with impossible odds; yet without delay or distraction, he finished the work of rebuilding the city (see Neh. 6:15). Nehemiah faced Sanballat and Tobiah, his first opposition, as will every city leader. There will always be Sanballats and Tobiahs!

> When Sanballat the Horonite and Tobiah the Ammonite official heard of it, they were deeply disturbed that a man had come to seek the well-being of the children of Israel (Neh. 2:10).

Nehemiah resisted the opposition and continued with his eye on the vision: rebuild the city. Don't let the enemy use people as distractions to get you off course. Stay on course with your eye on the goal—the city. Nehemiah was able to unite the people of God to work together in the reaching of the city. In Nehemiah 3, the leaders were united together in order to rebuild the city.

The key phrases in Nehemiah 3 are "next to," "next to them," and "next to him." These words indicate that a team spirit existed as they built the city. Every leader had a part of the city to work on, and every leader had a specific responsibility. The leaders were knit together in one spirit, one vision and one heart. All was for the city, not their own personal gain, not their own houses; their only motivation was for the vision of a rebuilt city.

The City Church must work together to impact a city, every congregation building on different parts of the wall, every congregation standing next to, with, along side of, and together in our ministry to the city. The knitting together of the leaders' hearts is first, then the congregations' hearts, and finally a unified city ministry can take place. We must pray that the

The Church can change the city instead of the city

changing the Church.

Holy Spirit will touch the eyes of the City Church to see this vision of unified city ministries (see Matt. 9:29,30; Luke 24:31; Eph. 1:18). The Church can change the city instead of the city changing the Church.

CITY CHURCH PROCLAMATIONS

As a City Church, our desire to reach the city together necessitates City Church goals. The following are proclamations to make:

- As a City Church, our desire is to build strong and spiritually healthy local churches with spiritual armories so together we can penetrate the spiritual powers over our city.

  The Lord has opened His armory, and has brought out the weapons of His indignation; for this is the work of the Lord God of hosts in the land of the Chaldeans (Jer. 50:25).

- As a City Church, our desire is to reap the harvest God would grant us from our city metro area and region, using every means available or necessary to accomplish this.

Then He said to His disciples, "The harvest truly is plentiful, but the laborers are few. Therefore pray the Lord of the harvest to send out laborers into His harvest" (Matt. 9:37,38).

- As a City Church, our desire is to mobilize all believers throughout our city and region to pray, fast, prayer-walk and unite together to minister mercy to every house, apartment and business within our targeted area, thus reaching our whole city.

He who sins is of the devil, for the devil has sinned from the beginning. For this purpose the Son of God was manifested, that He might destroy the works of the devil (1 John 3:8).

- As a City Church, our desire is to penetrate every pocket or stronghold of darkness by increasing our repentance, first denying all sins revealed and then increasing our power of prayer intercession over our city and region (see Gen. 18:22,23; Isa. 59:16).

So I sought for a man among them who would make a wall, and stand in the gap before Me on behalf of the land, that I should not destroy it; but I found no one (Ezek. 22:30).

- As a City Church, our desire is to help restore the inner city by reaching individuals with the gospel of Christ, seeing authentic conversions that result in new lifestyles, new life habits and rebuilding inner City Churches that will reap and keep the harvest.

Those from among you shall build the old waste places; you shall raise up the foundations of many generations; and you shall be called the Repairer of the Breach, the Restorer of Streets to Dwell In (Isa. 58:12).

• As a City Church, our desire is to oppose abortion, moral perversity, homosexuality, pornography, prostitution (all moral sins that violate God's laws) by being salt and light with political involvement as is necessary, taking responsibility for our city region laws, not by political activism only, but by aggressive intercession.

Son of man, I have made you a watchman for the house of Israel; therefore hear a word from My mouth, and give them warning from Me (Ezek. 3:17).

Ted Haggard speaks wisely in his book *Primary Purpose* about Christians and political involvement:

I believe that as responsible citizens, Christians should be involved in political issues. Even though we will be divided on most issues, there will be times when we will stand together. Some battles we will win, others we will lose. But the battle that must not be lost is the eternal struggle to liberate individuals spiritually, which will result in inspiring the whole community. In the midst of any political situation, we must stay steady and keep focused on our primary purpose, making it hard to go to hell from our cities.[3]

- As a City Church, our desire is to reach each generation with the power of the gospel, reaching past, present and future generations with relevant spiritual tools and methods, we commit to raising up young leadership who will take significant leadership roles in reaching our city region.

Now when Abram heard that his brother was taken captive, he armed his three hundred and eighteen trained servants who were born in his own house, and went in pursuit as far as Dan (Gen. 14:14).

- As a City Church, our desire is to be knit together as one corporate, unified spiritual net making up the City Church, a network of covenantal relationships governed by covenantal relationships that will catch a great amount of fish, but the net won't break.

Now I plead with you, brethren, by the name of our Lord Jesus Christ, that you all speak the same thing, and that there be no divisions among you, but that you be perfectly joined together in the same mind and in the same judgment (1 Cor. 1:10).

From whom the whole body, joined and knit together by what every joint supplies, according to the effective working by which every part does its share, causes growth of the body for the edifying of itself in love (Eph. 4:16).

Again, the kingdom of heaven is like a dragnet that was cast into the sea and gathered some of every kind (Matt. 13:47).

• As a City Church, our desire is to turn the tide of wickedness to righteousness. We desire a full-blown authentic revival to cover our city, resulting in new conversion growth in every Bible-believing, Jesus-centered church. We are believing that our prayers and presence will change the future of our city.

Cry aloud, spare not; lift up your voice like a trumpet; tell My people their transgression, and the house of Jacob their sins (Isa. 58:1).

Now then, we are ambassadors for Christ, as though God were pleading through us: we implore you on Christ's behalf, be reconciled to God (2 Cor. 5:20).

And I also say to you that you are Peter, and on this rock I will build My church, and the gates of Hades shall not prevail against it (Matt. 16:18).

For we do not wrestle against flesh and blood, but against principalities, against powers, against the rulers of the darkness of this age, against spiritual hosts of wickedness in the heavenly places (Eph. 6:12).

As a City Church consisting of many congregations, we have a great future if we will see the vision and work God's plan. The challenge far exceeds our ability to meet the needs, change the spiritual climate and reach every house for Christ. This is precisely why a prayer intercession revival is occurring right now. Intercession is the force that touches the heart that moves the hand that changes the world. Our cities can and will be reached by a powerful Christ who is lord over the city. Let us begin with prayer:

Father,

In the Name of Jesus, let Thy Kingdom come, let Thy will be done in our cities and regions. We stand against the spirits that are warring against our Portland/Vancouver region. We bind the spirits of rebellion, religious deception, blasphemy, immorality and witchcraft. Father God, release Your warring angels and release the Holy Spirit to do warfare against these enemies. Set this region free; establish Your rule and reign in our cities. Cause revival fires to burn hot in Your church. Send revival to this region. Release a spirit of repentance. Fill your church with compassion and mercy. Let the spirit of prayer intercession rest upon all congregations. Let us, by Your grace, make a difference in our generation. In Jesus' mighty name, we pray.

Amen.

Lord of the Harvest
By Sharon Damazio and Eugene Greco

Lord of the Harvest,
I hear You calling to me:
"Look out upon the fields,
They're ready to reap.
Whom can I send
And who will go for Me?
Will you answer, 'yes,'
Will you go to those in need?"

Lord of the Harvest,
I will go.
Remove the hardness
I find within my soul.
So many lives that are broken
With hearts wounded and torn;
How we need Your Spirit
To comfort those who mourn.

Lord of the Harvest,
I hear You calling to me:
"Give me your heart and soul,
Surrender to Me."
Not my will but Yours,
O Lord, I seek.
I will answer, "yes,"
Here I am, O Lord, use me.

Lord of the Harvest,
I will go.
Remove the hardness
I find within my soul.
Give me a heart of compassion
To feel somebody's pain;
Reaching out with mercy,
With your amazing grace.[4]

PERSONAL APPLICATION

1. Do you love your city? How concerned have you been
   with the crime, social issues and laws there? Have you
   ever considered praying through your city's phone

book or praying through the headlines of your local newspaper?

2. Do you have a Nehemiah attitude? Do you pray, fast, weep and mourn over your city? If not, will you commit to a set time each month for prayer with fasting over your city?

3. Are you a part of a City Church? If not, will you initiate one? If so, will you begin to declare the City Church proclamations presented in this chapter?

Notes

1. Ted Haggard, *Primary Purpose* (Lake Mary, FL: Creation House, 1995), p. 76.
2. Ted Haggard and Jack W. Hayford, *Loving Your City into the Kingdom* (Ventura, CA: Regal Books, 1997), p. 14.
3. Ted Haggard, *Primary Purpose* (Lake Mary, FL: Creation House, 1995), p. 51.
4. Sharon Damazio and Eugene Greco, "Lord of the Harvest," City Bible Music and His Banner Publishing, 1997. Used with permission.